WELSH RAREBITS

Bite-sized chunks of Welsh humour

D0474637

WELSH RAREBITS

Bite-sized chunks of Welsh humour

Aubrey Malone

y Lolfa

First impression: 2013

© Aubrey Dillon-Malone & Y Lolfa Cyf., 2013

Cover picture: Rianne Rowlands

ISBN: 978 1 84771 640 8

FSC

Published and printed in Wales
on paper from well maintained forests by
Y Lolfa Cyf., Talybont, Ceredigion SY24 5HE
e-mail ylolfa@ylolfa.com
website www.ylolfa.com
tel 01970 832 304
fax 832 782

INTRODUCTION

This anthology contains the essence of Welsh humour in all its wildness and eccentricity. Most of the usual suspects are here, with some new ones added. I've tried to keep it as contemporary as I could while preserving the older voices. I've also given priority to people who cut to the chase in their ruminations.

There's more to Wales than the three Rs: rugby, rain and religion. Having said that, such old faithfuls are present and correct here, as well as speculations on music, alcohol, the mines and anything else that makes the country throb.

It was hard not to draw heavily on people like Dylan Thomas and Richard Burton because they're so eminently quotable. With these luminaries and others we get acerbic putdowns, daft definitions, controversial insights, gaffes, prejudices, hoary old gags and some quirky philosophical reflections. I hope the whole is greater than the sum of the parts in shedding light on an often maligned and frequently misunderstood nation.

Expostulations range across the political and sporting divides as well. Some of the quotes are from non-Welsh people talking about Wales, or from those whose Welshness goes back a bit.

The beauty of an anthology is that it's often a spur to further reading. If you enjoy a one-liner it might cause you to dig deeper, even into a biography or autobiography. If this book does that it will have served its purpose. Fasten your seatbelts for a rollercoaster ride through life, love and the whole damn thing.

Aubrey Malone
June 2013

ACTORS AND ACTING

It's easier to cast an ethnic or disabled actor than a Welsh one.

KARL FRANCIS

Acting taught me a lot. What it taught me is that it is not for me.

RACHEL ROBERTS

Acting was something they did in between fighting, slurring their words and falling over. Usually their *parts* involved fighting, slurring their words and falling over as well – which, considering the amount of research they'd put in, they managed to do very, very badly.

A.A. GILL *on Richard Burton and Oliver Reed*

Method acting means taking on the personality of the person you're playing in your life. Thankfully Anthony Hopkins didn't do this for *Silence of the Lambs* or a few attractive women with big knockers would have disappeared under a parsley garnish.

JO BRAND

Half the fun of playing other parts is getting away from your own disgusting self.

RICHARD BURTON

Richard Burton acts with his voice.

JAY COCKS

Everyone acts. The only difference is some of us get paid for it.

DONALD HOUSTON

It's not the acting that's the work – it's the waiting ground between takes.

HUGH GRIFFITH

I hate talking about acting because I don't know what I'm doing half the time.

ANTHONY HOPKINS

Acting certainly beats working for a living.

JONATHAN PRYCE

Catherine's greatest performance of her career was when she played a chef. Because she can't boil water.

MICHAEL DOUGLAS *on his wife Catherine Zeta-Jones*

There should be an interaction between the actor and the audience. In a sense it should be as if the actor had just stepped out of the audience.

DIC EDWARDS

The only interesting parts to play are defeated men. Heroes are always faintly boring.

RICHARD BURTON

I used to be a very good actress... and then I married Rex Harrison.

RACHEL ROBERTS

I don't worry about the critics – unless one of them managed to act me off the screen.

HUGH GRIFFITH

I've never had much truck with Method acting. I just try to show up on time and remember my lines.

STANLEY BAKER

I became an actor to escape from myself.

HYWEL BENNETT

Quitting Hollywood is the beginning of maturity.

GLYNIS JOHNS

I lost interest in acting when people started talking about 'film' instead of 'films'.

DONALD HOUSTON

It's easier to play a psychopath than an ordinary person.

CHRISTIAN BALE

The main pressures in acting don't come from work. They come from not working.

RUFUS SEWELL

You never get to be a great actor until you're dead.

RICHARD BURTON

Most Hollywood affairs are between an actor and himself.

DAVID MCCALLUM

Somebody asked me the other day, 'How do you prepare?' I said 'I don't know. I just learn the lines and show up.'

ANTHONY HOPKINS

Richard Burton doesn't act; he recites.

MONTGOMERY CLIFT

The main difference between living in Wales and L.A. is that I now get to read scripts in a hot tub instead of a damp flat.

IOAN GRUFFUDD

Elizabeth Taylor carries around with her a cornucopian make-up case that Jupiter might have envied. It seems to contain endless things: eyebrow pencils, pens, deodorants, perfumes and what seem to be pills for any diseases and balms and elixirs and you name it. It may even contain spare parts for the Rolls.

RICHARD BURTON

When I was young I used to love the way actresses smelt. I didn't realise until years later that it was gin.

RHYS IFANS

I was destined to be an actor. The day I was born I stood up and took a bow. When the doctor slapped me, I thought it was applause.

BOB HOPE

Genevieve Bujold has all the power of a dying gnat. I could whisper louder than she screams.

RICHARD BURTON

Once a pass has been made in a football game, run into an open space for a return. Don't stand admiring your handiwork.

ROY PAUL

Never ask an English person for directions. They're too polite to tell you if they don't know the way, and will send you somewhere else instead – usually Wales.

JOE O'CONNOR

The best way to keep your hair from filling out is to knot it from the inside.

KEN DODD

Don't make jokes at the European Parliament. You'll find the Germans only get them ten minutes after the Swedes.

GLENYS KINNOCK

Never look at other women after you get married. Keep your eyes closed as you're making love to them.

HUW PHILIPS

The best way to make Welshmen behave is not to give them too much time to think.

EVELYN WAUGH

If you're going to stalk someone, the best person to pick is another stalker. He'll understand you. There won't be any awkward silences if you ring him after midnight. I once stalked a stalker who stalked a stalker who stalked another stalker. It worked out at quite a tally. We organised a minibus to go on outings.

RHOD GILBERT

Look at the bright side of unemployment. When you wake up in the morning, you're already at work.

TOMMY COOPER

'If you don't want to get your tyres slashed, don't wear GB plates,' was advice frequently given before our intended journey. We hoped to receive favourable treatment by announcing ourselves to be Welsh.

RICHARD BOOTH *on an imminent trip from England to Ireland*

Always shit on the English side of the bridge.

CARDIFF CHANT

The main problem with Paul McKenna's advice is that it comes from Paul McKenna.

KEITH BARRET

Don't become a playwright. It will make you become prematurely silly.

EMLYN WILLIAMS

My advice to all who want to attend a lecture on music is, 'Don't. Go to a concert instead.'

RALPH VAUGHAN WILLIAMS

I'm all in favour of keeping dangerous weapons out of the hands of fools. Let's start with typewriters.

FRANK LLOYD WRIGHT

Never buy what you do not want because it is cheap; it will be dear to *you*.

THOMAS JEFFERSON

Whether day of happiness come or not, one should try and prepare oneself to do without it.

GEORGE ELIOT

Streets flooded. Please advise.

ROBERT BENCHLEY *in a telegram after arriving in Venice*

Revenge is a dish best served cold.

DENNIS PRICE

If you rest on your laurels, they tend to become wreaths.

HARRY SECOMBE

I would advise anyone coming to the match to arrive early and not leave until the end. Otherwise they might miss something.

JOHN TOSHACK

Be careful with sound advice. Sometimes it's 99 per cent sound and just 1 per cent advice.

ROY NOBLE

If you're nervous about facing thousands of strangers, look at them as you would if you were looking over the hedge at a field of cabbages.

Advice given to **DAI JONES** *by the stage manager of a San Francisco concert*

Never live in a house next door to your landlady or landlord.

W.H. DAVIES

Never borrow money from an optimist. He always expects it back.

ALUN WILLIAMS

All teenagers should kill themselves.

RICHEY EDWARDS

Never do anything that you would be afraid to do in the last hour of your life.

JONATHAN EDWARDS

Better to be thought a fool than to speak out and remove all doubt.

ABRAHAM LINCOLN

If you're going to get wasted, get wasted elegantly.

KEITH RICHARDS

For God's sake stop dyeing your hair. It looks like someone's slung a bucket of soot on your head.

TOM JONES'S WIFE LINDA

If you can't stand the heat in the dressing room, get out of the kitchen.

TERRY VENABLES

The best thing a goalkeeper can do when he goes on the field is be prepared to fail.

NEVILLE SOUTHALL

Before you let the sun in, mind it wipes its shoes.

DYLAN THOMAS

If it should ever be your misfortune to have spent Sunday in Wales, always get to windward when the chapels are disgorging the faithful.

ARTHUR JOHNSON

If ever you go to Dolgelley
Don't stay at the Lion Hotel
There's nothing to put in your belly
And no one to answer the bell.

ANON

If you can't get poetry to read, you must write it.

SAUNDERS LEWIS

Take my advice and stay out of Wales, even if you're the prince of it.

JEFFREY BERNARD

I don't give advice. The last time I tried it, my player ended up on the top of a TV tower.

IAN WOOSNAM

If you want a thing done, get a couple of old broads to do it.

BETTE DAVIS

Don't be afraid to take a big step. You can't cross a chasm in two small jumps.

DAVID LLOYD GEORGE

Never depend on immersion in another person for your growth, for that other person is merely preying on you to create their own.

CAITLIN THOMAS

Beware the tyranny of the weak. They will suck you dry.

ANTHONY HOPKINS

If you want to look nicer, get dimmer switches installed in your house.

CAROL VORDERMAN

My dad gave me this advice: 'Save a pound if you earn two pounds. Never eat fish on Mondays and never play snooker with a left-handed Welsh miner.'

TED RAY

AGE AND AGEING

No one will ever know when to give me a gold watch.

BARRY JOHN

I want to retire at 50. I want to play cricket and geriatric football and sing in the choir.

NEIL KINNOCK

Poets are thought of by the public as being forever young. Mr X, though he may be over 40, is always described as 'one of Britain's young poets'. Even when he's the funeral side of 50, he's still likely to be called 'One of Britain's younger poets'.

DANNIE ABSE

If by the time we're 60 we haven't learned what a knot of paradox life is and how exquisitely the good and bad are mingled in every action we take, we haven't grown old to much purpose.

JOHN COWPER POWYS

You want to know how I spent my 70th birthday? I put on a completely black face, a fuzzy black Afro wig, wore black clothes and hung a black wreath on my door.

BETTE DAVIS

A Welshman at 20 is either an awkward edition of 50 or else he's gone English.

ALUN OWEN

A woman could never be president of America. Candidates must be over 35 and where are you going to find a woman who'll admit to that?

BOB HOPE

Far from becoming more spiritual as I have gotten older, I have become a caterwauling virago of fanatical materialism.

CAITLIN THOMAS

A woman stopped me on the street one day and said, 'Excuse me, didn't you once used to be Cary Grant?'

CARY GRANT

One thing that reinforces my fear of flying is that you never see an old stewardess.

MAX BOYCE

I don't generally feel anything until noon. Then it's time for my nap.

BOB HOPE

I once tried to join the Young Communist Party but I was too old.

DYLAN THOMAS

Some golfing legends have been around a long time. When they mention a good grip, they're talking about their dentures.

BOB HOPE

A woman is as young as her knees.

MARY QUANT

You know you're getting old when the candles cost more than the cake.

BOB HOPE

Why, Lord, did you make Cwm Pennant so lovely and the life of an old shepherd so short?'

ELISEUS WILLIAMS

Tom Jones has discovered the secret of perpetual middle age.

IFOR WILLIAMS

One of my dearest friends is 84 but still looks shocked every time someone offers her a seat on the bus or tries to help her cross the road.

SIÂN MICHAELS

Dafydd once told his son that if he wanted to live a long life, the secret was to sprinkle a little gunpowder on his cornflakes every morning. The son did this religiously and lived to be 93. When he died he left 14 children, 28 grandchildren, and a 15-foot hole in the wall of the crematorium.

MILES JEFFREYS

I'll be around until the green, green grass of home is turned into a car park.

TOM JONES

I have fought for my living from an age when most kids would have blubbed if they had been spanked until an age when I should have known better.

TOMMY FARR

My parents never told me anything about sex but I got the distinct feeling my father didn't want me to date until a reasonable age – say 30 or so.

MARLENE MASON

Age is a state of mind. If you're 60 now and there had been 15 months in every year, you'd only be 48.

ROY NOBLE

Old age is worth it when you consider the alternative.

BETTE DAVIS

As you get older you become less horny. I don't take as many cold showers a day now as I used to.

TOM JONES

You don't get older, you get better.

SHIRLEY BASSEY

I always knew it was my age that made me special. If I'd been 35 with the same voice I'd probably have been earning my living as a mediocre soprano.

CHARLOTTE CHURCH

Last month Catherine Zeta-Jones raised a few eyebrows with her flirty behaviour with veteran actor Sean Connery, a man old enough to be her husband.

MARTIN CLUNES

ANIMALS

I once contemplated suicide. I took my shotgun into the woods but then my little dog licked my nose. He broke me out of it.

VINNIE JONES

I've been nominated for an Oscar and now he wants me to lip-synch a parrot's voice.

RACHEL ROBERTS *on Rex Harrison's humiliating offer to her while he was filming Dr Doolittle*

There was a chapel deacon in Monmouthshire who was devastated by the passing of his black cat. In an attempt to provide some kind of life after death he had the creature skinned and made into a sleek binding for his Bible. The tail, still attached, was used as a page marker.

TREVOR FISHLOCK

The Welsh have invented a new use for sheep. Wool.

MILES JEFFREYS

To live in Wales is to love sheep and be afraid of dragons.

PETER FINCH

A boy can learn a lot from a dog – obedience, loyalty, and the importance of turning around three times before lying down.

ROBERT BENCHLEY

John Wayne's horse will one day be vice-president of the United States.

GWYN THOMAS

The local education authority sent me to Garw Grammar School. Sheep were often to be seen wandering through the schoolyards. Occasionally they would attempt to graze in the classrooms.

HOWARD MARKS

I do not believe that any peacock envies another peacock his tail because every peacock believes his own one is the finest in the world. The consequence of this is that peacocks are peaceable birds.

BERTRAND RUSSELL

Betting is the manure to which the enormous crop of horse races and racehorse breeding in this and other countries is to a large extent due.

RICHARD BLACKMORE

My horse finished so far back, the jockey had to run ahead of him with a flashlight.

BOB HOPE

A ewe, the property of Mr W. Tatham of Aberystwyth, has presented its owner with quadrupeds.

Report in **SOUTH WALES ECHO**

Motoring tourist: 'I'm sorry I ran over your hen. If I give you £5, will that be all right?'
Cardi farmer: 'Better make it £10. I've got a cockerel that was very attached to that hen and the shock might kill him as well.'

CHRISTIE DAVIES

I used to wrestle with tigers in a circus.

> **TOMMY FARR** *to Joe Louis when Louis asked him where he got some cuts he had on his face*

I backed a horse at 20 to 1. It came in at 20 past 4.

TOMMY COOPER

We lived in a house in Anglesey. It was so small the mice were re-accommodated by the council.

BILL SHIPTON

Q. What's a Welsh farmer's best defence in court?

A. 'Honest, Your Honour, I was just helping the sheep over the fence.'

INTERNET JOKE

There must be gorillas so bemused by the warm testimonials written for them by anthropologists that they stand shyly in their jungles wondering what gift to expect – a hand of bananas or a clutch of Nobel prizes.

GWYN THOMAS

Getting a pet might be a way of humanising yourself but a Labrador won't fool me.

KEN FOLLETT *on Peter Mandelson*

I went to the dentist. He said 'Say Aaah.' I said 'Why?' He said, 'My dog died.'

TOMMY COOPER

David Attenborough is a TV bloke who goes around in a safari suit telling us how bloody great animals are. He forgets it wasn't an animal who invented the TV – or the safari suit.

DAVID BADDIEL

You can't say to your cat, 'Stay', 'Wait', 'Lie' or 'Roll over'. It would just be sitting there going, 'Interesting words. Have you finished?'

EDDIE IZZARD

Animals kill each other viciously. I have no objections to man joining the fray.

RICHARD BOOTH

When children ape adults, even the apes complain.

GWYN THOMAS

He wasn't a poet at all, just a Welsh alley cat screaming.

BRENDAN BEHAN *on Dylan Thomas*

What do you get if you cross a sheep with a Border collie? A dog that rounds up Welshmen.

MILES JEFFREYS

What would you call a Welshman with a sheep under each arm? A pimp.

INTERNET JOKE

Animal testing is totally unfair. They all get nervous and give the wrong answers.

GWILYM EVANS

A day is the length of a gnat's life. I want you for the lifetime of a big, mad animal.

DYLAN THOMAS *to Caitlin in a letter*

Safe sex in north Wales means branding the sheep that kicks.

VICTOR LEWIS-SMITH

The pig lies down in dung to sleep because dung is warm and soft. He would probably think it a very dirty thing indeed to sleep on a sheet.

DYLAN THOMAS

BEHAVIOUR

I never turned blue in somebody else's bathroom. I consider that the height of bad manners.

KEITH RICHARDS

Did you ever see your wife messing with her hair and going, 'It's not doing what I want it to do?' It's hair, love. What do you expect it to do – line dance?

LEE EVANS

A good night on the town for me involves lawyers and paramedics.

RHYS IFANS

Next to enjoying ourselves, the next greatest pleasure consists in preventing others from doing so.

BERTRAND RUSSELL

Welsh women are shrewd in the marketplace, devout in chapel, and frantic in bed.

ANON

Men move dimly towards what in their essence they wish to become. The things that happen to them have already been planted by them in the waiting darkness ahead.

GWYN THOMAS

Charles Boyer kissed with his mouth open but he was French. Was this the way to do it?

HUGH LOUDON *on watching movies as a child in Pontypridd*

How a Welshman behaves towards you depends on whether or not you belong to any of the groups with which he is in conflict at the moment. If you happen to be in one such proscribed group, be prepared for anything up to and including single combat.

JOHN RICHARDS

Look closely at any man who has made himself absolutely clear and you will see that he has become a little more sinister.

GWYN THOMAS

Women always send their most important letter news in postscripts.

SAUNDERS LEWIS

I like to shout regularly at the players around me. It reminds them that I'm still alive.

NEVILLE SOUTHALL

I learned a lot in the *Big Brother* house. For instance, I'm now able to boil an egg.

GLYN WISE

Gavin Henson didn't take too kindly to being left out of the Lions squad in 2005. Some claim he now holds the official world record for slamming doors without quite detaching them from their hinges.

JAMES LAWTON

When I told my mother I was playing a gay bingo caller in a TV show she said, 'Well make sure you don't tell anyone you're a bingo caller!'

KEVIN JOHNS

I condition my hair with beer and honey and smell like a brewery for days afterwards.

CATHERINE ZETA-JONES

Once during my hairdressing days I cut a customer's necklace off.

HELEN ADAMS

One must live in the present tense but I have always lived in the present tensely.

BETTE DAVIS

Dylan read everything, even the backs of sauce bottles.

CAITLIN THOMAS

I rarely stop talking. How can I know what I think until I hear what I say?

HUW WHELDON

Ken Loach's *Abigail's Party* was so unbearably real I had to watch it from behind the sofa.

JANET STREET-PORTER

Hysteria, like everything else, comes with practice.

CAITLIN THOMAS

I'm Jones the Voice. It's what I do. They'll be nailing down my coffin and I'll still be belting out a tune.

TOM JONES

I've sung for the Pope, the Queen and the President of America but I'm happiest mucking about the house.

CHARLOTTE CHURCH

It's strange, isn't it? You stand in the middle of a library and go 'Aaaaarrrgh!' and everyone just stares at you. But do the same thing on a plane and they all join in.

TOMMY COOPER

BIRTH

They tell me my arrival on this earth coincided with George Best walking out on Manchester United for the last time.

RYAN GIGGS

I was relieved when Tony Blair's baby was born at the Chelsea and Westminster Hospital. I had thought it would have been in a manger.

LEO ABSE

Tommy Cooper's father wanted his child to be born in Wales so that if it turned out to be male he would be eligible to play rugby for the country.

JEREMY NOVICK

My father said the day I was born was a red letter day. He received final demands for the gas, the electricity, and half a dozen assorted HP items.

TOMMY COOPER

The reason I was born in Wales is because I wanted to be near my mother.

MAX BOYCE

Swansea bore me but I have also bored Swansea.

DYLAN THOMAS

One isn't born a Welshwoman. One becomes one.

KATE BURGESS

I was born in Wales 33 years ago, the product of love between a man, a woman, and some lousy television reception.

BILL SHIPTON

If I were reincarnated I would wish to be returned to Earth as a killer virus to lower human population levels.

PRINCE PHILIP

When I was born my mother stole the limelight by having an asthma attack.

CHARLOTTE CHURCH

At birth when a Welshman is slapped on the behind he doesn't cry. Instead he sings 'Men of Harlech' in perfect pitch.

ALAN JAY LERNER

I was a surprise to my parents. They found me on the doorstep. They were expecting a bottle of milk.

TOMMY COOPER

We're born in other people's pain and perish in our own.

DYLAN THOMAS

BOOKS

There are two motives for reading a book. One, that you enjoy it. Two, that you can boast about it.

BERTRAND RUSSELL

I'm not that happy with my game. Maybe I should read my book to get some ideas.

IAN WOOSNAM, *the author of* Power Golf

A good book is a man's best friend, and a lantern.

EVAN EVANS

I bought 1,000 copies of an out-of-date accountancy book and 80 tons of *The Initial Teaching Alphabet*, an anticipated educational breakthrough which ended up as a lorry-load of scrap.

Second-hand book dealer **RICHARD BOOTH**

This is just the book to give to your sister, if she's a loud, dirty, boozy girl.

DYLAN THOMAS *on Flann O'Brien's* At-Swim-Two-Birds.

I would write books even if they were only read by my husband.

AGATHA CHRISTIE

I used to think that romantic paperbacks were written in the same way as Mickey Spillane novels, for which undergraduates were given a few pounds to write lines like, 'He opened the door and she had nothing on but the radio'.

RICHARD BOOTH

My father had a wonderful phrase: 'Never judge a book by its cover.' Although if I was being picky I would have to say that the cover is probably the best way to judge a book. *Coastal Walks in Pembrokeshire*, for example, is almost definitely a guide to the many lovely walks that are available along the Pembrokeshire coast, and not, I would wager, the story of one man's struggle against apartheid in South Africa.

KEITH BARRET

If a law were passed giving six months in jail to every writer of a first book, literature would be spared many an embarrassment.

BERTRAND RUSSELL

It's untrue that I prefer broads to books. I now read four or five books a day. It's a long time (pre-Elizabethan as a matter of fact) since I had four broads in a day – and even then they were little more than punctuation marks.

RICHARD BURTON

My wife's favourite book is the chequebook. Once she picks it up she finds it difficult to put it down again.

HARRY SECOMBE

Is it a book you would wish your wife – or even your servants – to read?

Lawyer **MERVYN GRIFFITH-JONES** *at the* Lady Chatterley's Lover *trial*

Geri Halliwell has now published two volumes of her autobiography. That means she's already written as many books as God. Or, if you're Jewish, twice as many.

MARK WATSON

Did you hear about the library scissors? It was a real turn-up for the books.

TOMMY COOPER

BOREDOM

Robert Owen may be described as one of those intolerable bores who are the salt of the earth.

LESLIE STEPHEN

Authors have the power to bore people long after we're dead.

SINCLAIR LEWIS

A speech from Ernest Bevin on a major occasion had all the fascination of a public execution.

MICHAEL FOOT

When you're bored with yourself, marry and be bored with someone else.

DAVID PRYCE-JONES

People who in 1877 would have walked over 20 miles of moorland to listen to Gladstone outlining his portrait of the New Jerusalem now yawn or chuckle in bored incredulity as they listen to the political telecast that tells them Britain's troubles are on the mend.

GWYN THOMAS

When I watch matches these days I reckon five out of every six are drab and downright boring.

BARRY JOHN

There is no play or film that I've ever been in that hasn't bored me after about six weeks.

RICHARD BURTON

A bore and a bounder and a prig. He was intoxicated with his own youth and loathed any milieu he couldn't dominate. Certainly he had none of the gentleman's instincts, strutting about peace conferences in Arab dress.

SIR HENRY CHANNON *on* T.E. *Lawrence*

Being famous means you can bore people and they think it's their fault.

DAI JENKINS

A nincompoop once described meeting Dylan Thomas to me: 'He allowed me to do all the talking. Leaning with one elbow on the bar counter, he raised his eyes to the ceiling. They were slightly glazed and I knew that, undisturbed by my words, genius was even then at work in him.' I did not mention in reply that I knew well what that glazed look meant. It meant: 'How much can I touch this bloody bore for?'

DAN JONES

Richard Burton can entertain you nonstop for three weeks but in the fourth he starts to repeat himself.

JULIE ANDREWS

By remaining sober for the last three or four days I have learned a great deal. I had forgotten how boring people are. I had forgotten how boring *I* am.

RICHARD BURTON

CARDIS

A Cardi is a man who can buy an item from a Jew, sell it to a Scotsman and still make a profit.

Did you hear about the Cardi farmer who stuck a mirror to his dog's feeding bowl to make him think he was getting two bones for his dinner?

Cardis buy anything marked down – including escalators.

A Cardi found a plaster one day. He cut his finger so he could use it.

Cardi Catholics claim that they invested St Patrick in the Bank of Ireland over 1,500 years ago and are now drawing interest in Irish priests working in Wales.

Did you hear about the Cardi who did the smash and grab in Cardiff? He would have got away with it if he didn't go back for the brick.

Cardi farmers get married in their farmyards so they can keep the rice.

If a Cardi gives you a compliment he asks for a receipt.

A Cardi was out walking one night when a mugger thrust a knife in his face. 'Your money or your life!' the mugger said. 'I'm thinking,' the Cardi replied.

Then there was the Cardi farmer who never lit a fire even in the middle of winter. Instead he used to suck a humbug and the rest of the family would sit around his tongue.

A Cardi is a man who only cries over spilt milk if there's a water shortage.

Cardis are surprised about the fact that, despite the cost of living, it's still very popular.

Cardi girls still believe the best labour-saving device is a husband with money.

A Cardi was stripping his wallpaper. A friend walked in on him. 'I see you're decorating,' he said. 'No', the Cardi replied, 'Moving'.

Visitor to Cardi seaside resort: 'I want to buy a toothbrush.' Shopkeeper: 'I'm sorry but our summer novelties haven't come in yet.'

I bought my son an Arsenal shirt from Jack Kelsey's shop, ensuring that by doing so I would get to talk to Jack. As I wrote out my cheque he casually asked me where I was from. When I told him Aberystwyth he threw my cheque on the counter to make sure it didn't bounce. Then he held it up to the light. 'You can never tell with you bloody Cardis,' he quipped.

LYN EBENEZER

CHILDREN AND CHILD-HOOD

There are children from sane, functional families who turn out to be monstrous f***-ups, and children from what are considered to be textbook dysfunctional families that turn out OK.

SOPHIE DAHL

I very much like children telling me about their childhood but they have to be quick or else I'll be telling them about mine.

DYLAN THOMAS

You've never been a parent until you've been hated by your child.

BETTE DAVIS

When I was a little boy I wanted to be like Shirley Bassey.

BOY GEORGE

My mother was one of the original Welsh mums who would say to me when I was a child climbing trees, 'If you fall and break your legs, don't come running to me.'

KEVIN JOHNS

The fundamental defect of fathers in our competitive society is that they want their children to be a credit to them.

BERTRAND RUSSELL

In America there are two classes of travel: first class, and with children.

ROBERT BENCHLEY

There's only one thing worse than having an unhappy childhood and that's having a too happy childhood.

DYLAN THOMAS

As a girl I wanted to be an air hostess because people don't finish their meals on planes and I could scoff all the leftovers behind the secret curtains.

DAWN FRENCH

Every Saturday morning I had to take piano lessons from a teacher called Professor Balaclava Evans. He was born during a period when it was fashionable to name children after famous battles and heroic generals. There was even a kid in our school named Khartoum Harris.

RAY MILLAND

The first thing I can properly remember is having breathing competitions with my father.

GRIFF RHYS JONES

I was abused by my father and mother separately with strict injunctions from both not to tell the other. Later they hired me out to other people for hours at a time. At eleven I wasn't sure if I was still a child but I knew I was a whore.

CERIDWEN HUGHES

As a child I wanted to be just like my mother; now I want the similarity to end in the mirror. The image I grew up with feels like a counterfeit and I'm struggling to find its original.

ANNA SWAN

My earliest memory is of throwing a cat into the deep ocean from the deck of a ship. Why did I do it? I swear that I expected the cat to go for a swim, catch fish, and return triumphantly.

HOWARD MARKS

I was five when the last bomb to fall on Cardiff destroyed our home.

STELLA LEVEY *on World War II*

In my childhood I saw more of Monument Valley than of Scotland and Wales.

CHARLES WAY

I was never a child. I was born a rock god.

DAVID BOWIE

The person I was as a child forms 90 per cent of my work.

ROALD DAHL

There were so many in my family, I was eight years old before it was my turn in the bathroom.

BOB HOPE

Growing up I was convinced the bogey man lived in our house. It was a nightmare going to the toilet. I'd look over my shoulder and check in the mirror that I hadn't gone missing.

KEVIN JOHNS

Will Charlotte Church have 'the voice of an angel' when she's woken up by her child at 3 a.m.?

MIKE HASKINS

My mother says I was able to sing before I could walk.

TOM JONES

One of my chief troubles is making money. Most of the little I make seems to go on my children, who persist in getting older all the time.

DYLAN THOMAS

The main reason children brighten a home is because they never turn off the bloody lights.

HARRY SECOMBE

To have grown up as an English-speaking Welsh child in Wales in the 1970s was to know the befuddled agony of staring at the TV screen as the continuity announcer declared, 'Now on BBC1, *Batman…* except for viewers in Wales', and a newsreader began, in his native tongue, bringing us up to speed with the latest developments in our homeland, a high proportion of which seemed to feature reporters in rain-swept fields addressing the camera to a herd of cows lolled around behind them.

ROB BRYDON

CLOTHING

Do you know why Michael [Douglas] doesn't do weights any more? Because he sacrificed his home gym for my closet. We have a StairMaster and stuff in there but the rest had to go. And the closet still isn't big enough.

CATHERINE ZETA-JONES

His appropriation of other people's assets had even led him, on one celebrated occasion, to steal a host's clothes.

ROB GITTINS *on Dylan Thomas*

I think I know this woman. I forget names, I forget faces, but there are some things I never forget.

TOM JONES *at a concert in Melbourne in 1990 after a pair of knickers were thrown onto the stage*

Dai came home from the pub one night after work. Mari said, 'Can I have some money? I want to buy a bra.' Dai replied, 'What for? You've got nothing to put in it'. Mari said, 'You wear pants, don't you?'

MILES JEFFREYS

We always had to change for dinner even when we dined 'à deux'.

ELIZABETH HARRISON *on her marriage to Rex*

I shall be bloody furious if I don't have a chance to show off my new dinner jacket.

RICHARD BURTON *on the Oscar ceremonies in 1970. He had been nominated for* Anne of a Thousand Days *but lost out to John Wayne for* True Grit

My ambition was always to create a kind of scrubbed simple beauty.

LAURA ASHLEY

We had a topless lady ventriloquist in Liverpool once. Nobody ever saw her lips move.

KEN DODD

Aprons are sexy, with or without clothes underneath. We all fantasise about a man in a pinny.

CATHERINE ZETA-JONES

It takes 40 dumb animals to make a fur coat but only one to wear it.

BRYN JONES

Don't judge Cher by her clothes. There isn't enough evidence.

BOB HOPE

I've got blouses with a bow at the neck like Margaret Thatcher because they're the only kind that fit me.

DAWN FRENCH

You can't wave your arms particularly high, and you also need help going to the toilet.

CHRISTIAN BALE *on donning the bat suit for* Batman Begins

Women have this vast variety of lingerie – stockings and tights and shoes with different-sized heels and skirts, long and short and with slits, push-the-boob things and so on. Men have shirt shirt shirt, jumper shirt jumper, jacket jumper shirt, jacket trousers trousers, shirt trousers flat shoes.

EDDIE IZZARD

I went to America to promote *The Man Who Sold the World*. As I was going through Texas I wore a dress. A guy pulled out a gun and called me a fag. But I thought the dress was beautiful.

DAVID BOWIE

Once only the rich set the fashion. Now it is the inexpensive little dress seen on the girls in the high street.

MARY QUANT

Our school uniform was a bottle-green gymslip with large pleats, tied like a sack in the middle, with a belt. Erotic it was not.

ANNE COLLEDGE

When we went to a party, Dylan would often leave with a better coat than the one he was wearing when he arrived.

CAITLIN THOMAS

The girls are wearing less and less on the beach now, which is perfect for me because my memory is starting to go.

BOB HOPE

My wife was looking through a fashion magazine and she saw a fur coat. She said 'I want that.' So I cut it out and gave it to her.

TOMMY COOPER

The typical Welsh intellectual is only one generation away from shirt-sleeves.

RAYMOND WILLIAMS

The bat suit makes you feel like a wild animal – you want to beat the shit out of people.

CHRISTIAN 'BATMAN' BALE

I'm a stripper at heart. I love taking my clothes off.

SHIRLEY BASSEY

I once spent £1,450 on underwear in a single shopping spree.

IMOGEN THOMAS, *the former Miss Wales*

He wouldn't have been seen dead in it.

ACQUAINTANCE OF DYLAN THOMAS *on his funeral garb*

I was voted Rear of the Year when I was 16 but now I'm so busy with my TV show I pig out on junk food between takes. I've got industrial strength gripper knickers to hide the flab. Thank you, Bridget Jones!

CHARLOTTE CHURCH

Photocopier toner is specially developed to run out only on the days when you're wearing your spanking new cream blouse. When you've finished ever so carefully changing it your blouse will look like a Welsh miner's donkey jacket.

GUY BROWNING

Who was the French poet who had alphabetically-lettered underpants, and wore ones up to 'H' on cold mornings?

DYLAN THOMAS

Jockeys are three-foot-high hobbits wearing pimps' clothing.

LEE EVANS

COMPARISONS

I wound down the window to ask a local character for directions. He obliged like the man who'd invented the compass.

GWYN THOMAS *after being lost in the Welsh hinterland*

Like the Welsh, we Irish also think we're great singers and artists. We've also spent millions trying to keep a dead language on life support – and we're no good at rugby either.

ANTHONY TORMEY

The *Big Brother* house is more luxurious than prison but less than Butlins.

MAGGOT, *a 2006 contestant on the show*

When Anthony Hopkins talks it's like being dusted with deeply perfumed talcum powder.

SALLY WEALE

A spa hotel is like a normal hotel, only in reception there's a picture of a pebble.

RHOD GILBERT

Goals have been my lifeblood for as long as I can remember. I eat them up as greedily as a starving man would wolf down a meal.

IAN RUSH

He held on to his Welsh background like a good cardinal holding on to his first hair shirt.

MELVYN BRAGG *on Richard Burton*

I pursued her like a heat-seeking missile.

MICHAEL DOUGLAS *on his early infatuation with Catherine Zeta-Jones*

I was growing disillusioned with an organisation that would commission expensive market research to see whether housewives would choose a Welsh holiday if given the chance to win a free fitted kitchen instead.

RICHARD BOOTH *on the Welsh Tourist Board*

When we were introduced I was shocked to feel her tiny, fleshless hand. It was like holding a bird's claw or a small cat's paw.

SIÂN PHILLIPS *on Audrey Hepburn*

Gavin Henson's hairstyle looks like a privet hedge cut by a drunk on steroids.

WYN JONES

Being married is like being at an auction. Think of your wife as the 'lot' for which you are bidding. If you've lost her to another, don't look on it as a rejection. You've simply been outbid.

KEITH BARRET

He looks like he's making love to fresh air.

GORDON MILLS *on Tom Jones's pelvic gyrations on stage*

Having starred with Clint Eastwood I cannot quite say it was a thespic experience on the order of Lunt and Fontaine acting together.

RICHARD BURTON

Steve Davis and Stephen Hendry play a different kind of snooker. Davis strangles you slowly.

TERRY GRIFFITHS

Whenever I look at John Charles it feels as though the Messiah has returned.

JIMMY MURPHY

The press can best be compared to haemorrhoids.
GARETH DAVIES

My mother was like an orchid among foxgloves.
ANNA SWAN

Gavin Henson and Charlotte Church make Posh and Becks look like something from *Brideshead Revisited*.
JAMES LAWTON

Dinner in the *Celebrity Jungle* camp was like Christmas in a mental ward.
JANET STREET-PORTER

Christmas is like Sunday with presents.
ANNA SNOW

Dylan was as useless as a penguin with his hands, except for one purpose.
CAITLIN THOMAS

If Zane Grey went out with a mosquito net to catch minnows he could make it sound like a Roman gladiator setting forth to slay whales in the Tiber.
ROBERT H. DAVIES

To hear Tom Jones sing Sinatra's 'My Way' is roughly akin to watching Tab Hunter play *King Lear*.
SHERIDAN MORLEY

I remember when I first saw Ryan Giggs. He was 13 and he just floated over the ground like a cocker spaniel chasing a piece of silver paper in the wind.
ALEX FERGUSON

S.J. Perelman writes like a Hollywood advertising copywriter after reading James Joyce, e.e. cummings and Sam Goldwyn's ace publicity stooge in a state of hypertension in a Turkish bath.

DYLAN THOMAS

F***ing basketball on grass now, innit?

VINNIE JONES *on the sad plight of 'the beautiful game' in 1999*

I first saw Peter O'Toole playing Edmund in *King Lear* at the Bristol Old Vic. He looked like a beautiful, emaciated secretary bird.

RICHARD BURTON

Ryan Giggs is another George Best? Maybe some day they'll be saying I was another Ryan Giggs.

GEORGE BEST

When I'm performing I'm like the guy who has a girl cornered in a hotel room with my body blocking the door. I not only suggest sex, I demand it.

TOM JONES

Richard Burton plays Henry VIII like a man who has promised to buy another diamond before Easter, using himself like an acting machine that will, if flogged, produce another million dollars.

PENELOPE MORTIMER *on Burton in* Anne of a Thousand Days

Today's youngsters play snooker as if they're having open heart surgery.

CLIFF WILSON

I slept like a log last night. Woke up in the fireplace.

TOMMY COOPER

Neil Kinnock has a certain amount of street cred. From a certain angle he looks like a Belisha beacon.

JERRY SADOWITZ

My father never slept like a baby. He slept like a piece of agricultural pumping machinery.

GRIFF RHYS JONES

Ian Rush was like Douglas Bader – great on the ground but useless in the air.

DAI GRIFFITHS

The problem with France is that, like Wales, it's a very pretty country spoiled only by the people who live there.

JEREMY CLARKSON

Susannah Constantine is a carthorse in a badly-fitting bin liner.

CAROL VORDERMAN

Carol Vorderman looks like mutton dressed as yak. The skirts that are an embarrassing innuendo, the come-and-get-me coiffure, the factor 97 make-up, the thickly sticky lips that look like she's been drinking warm chicken fat. The whole edifice is a desperate fanning of the dead embers of sensuality. There's a middle-aged woman who looks like this perched on the end of every wine bar in Cheshire.

A.A. GILL

Nothing is noisier than a philistine in pain.

JOHN OSBORNE

Hearing Tom Jones sing is like standing in a tunnel with an express train speeding towards you.

CERYS MATHEWS

I'd rather tickle the cheek of the English public than lick its arse.

DYLAN THOMAS

CONTRADICTIONS

My wife told me I disagree with everything she says. I said, 'No I don't'.

LEE EVANS

Wales is marching backwards into independence.

HARRI WEBB

Where were you going the other day when I saw you coming back?

DAVID JANDRELL

The claim to equality is made only by those who feel themselves to be in some way inferior.

C.S. LEWIS

The most innocent, wicked man I have ever met.

W.B. YEATS *on Augustus John*

You can have lovely shiny buttocks and guns everywhere in the supermarket, on covers of magazines and CDs, but show a piece of art and people just freak out.

JAMES DEAN BRADFIELD

When I played drunks I had to remain sober because I didn't know how to play them when I was drunk.

RICHARD BURTON

My insomnia is so bad I can't even sleep where I work.

TOMMY COOPER

The Welsh attitude to the English may be summed up as 10 per cent resentment and 90 per cent pity.

JOHN RICHARDS

There is no gaiety as gay as the gaiety of grief.

CAITLIN THOMAS

It took the English to make a Welshman of me.

NIGEL JENKINS

I'd like to give up writing but knowing me, if I did, I'd probably end up writing about it.

DYLAN THOMAS

The Irishmen I like best are not those who, like James Joyce, hate Ireland but cannot escape it. I suppose the reason is because I am a Welshman who hates Wales and yet cannot leave it.

SAUNDERS LEWIS

Richard Burton was Dylan Thomas as played by Casanova and directed by Mel Brooks.

ROBERT SELLERS

I know I am home again because I feel just as I felt when I was not at home, only more so.

DYLAN THOMAS

Richard Burton may have flown the Welsh dragon but for him it was always an exile's flag.

JOHN COTTRELL

If you're going to play a monster you should play him as attractively as possible.

ANTHONY HOPKINS *on Hannibal Lecter*

Dylan was very conscious of death but when his own time came he didn't practise what he preached. He slipped very gently into his good night.

CAITLIN THOMAS

It was odd; I would still have recurring dreams of winning the football pools even though I had more than the prize money lying idly under the bed.

HOWARD MARKS *on the cash he accumulated from smuggling drugs*

Even though I'm a multi-millionaire I'm a Communist at heart.

RICHARD BURTON

A fanatical belief in democracy makes democratic institutions impossible.

BERTRAND RUSSELL

I was stunned with outrage.

NEIL KINNOCK

Soccer is the greatest game in the world – and the worst. It encourages man to reach the supreme heights of athletic perfection yet it attracts some of the world's worst bums. It has a code of conduct designed to prevent corruption yet it does everything to encourage it. It's a game full of crooks for it's well-nigh impossible for a player to reach the top without breaking almost every law in the book.

TREVOR FORD

A typical road sign in rural Wales? 'Yes, You Can't.'

BARBARA ELLIS

I had lost and yet won.

TOMMY FARR *after his 'moral' victory against Joe Louis in the 1937 world championship bout*

Wales has never had a postmodernist age. This means that Welsh people can wear flowers, a red beach jumper, have spiky hair, listen to Margaret Williams and hymns and drop acid all at the same time without any contradictions.

EDWARD THOMAS

Why is the Prince of Wales not Welsh?

GLYN WISE *from* Big Brother 7

If I call my mum a nutter that's OK but if I heard someone else saying it I'd strangle them.

CHARLOTTE CHURCH

I wouldn't be at home if I was at home.

DYLAN THOMAS

CYNICISM

The inaccessibility of Aberystwyth to the outside world must be regarded as a dispensation of providence. Such a town deserves to be isolated.

THOMAS DAVIES

Practically the only growth industry in Wales has been the invention of its own history.

IAN SKIDMORE

Like a cushion, he always bore the impress of the last man who sat upon him.

DAVID LLOYD GEORGE *on Lord Derby*

There are no poets in Britain in jail for being subversive happily – though I dare say some ought to be for their lack of talent.

DANNIE ABSE

Harold Macmillan has a genius for putting flamboyant labels on empty luggage.

ANEURIN BEVAN

Diamonds never leave you. Men do.

SHIRLEY BASSEY

Soccer players are bought and sold like inorganic masonry, with the vendor and purchaser not even paying transfer-of-property tax.

TREVOR FORD

There's nothing more off-putting than 'new writing'. It means, 'Don't go to see that play, it will be crap'.

EDWARD THOMAS

In Wales we hail heroic losers. We seem unable to honour true champions.

BRYCHAN LLŶR

She's the sort of woman who lives for others. You can tell the others by their hunted expressions.

C.S. LEWIS

It's a long time since I was in Wales and I've loved every minute of it.

LES DAWSON

Actors are like sculptures in snow. In the end it's all nothing.

VINCENT PRICE

If we were given by magic the power to read each other's thoughts, I suppose the first effect would be to dissolve all friendships.

BERTRAND RUSSELL

Every human creature is a terror to every other human creature.

JOHN COWPER POWYS

Is Wales becoming nothing more than a nation of museum attendants? My Orwellian nightmare is a big black sign at the Severn Bridge saying 'You are now entering a protected industrial relic. Pay £5 to view this disappearing society.'

HYWEL FRANCIS

We eat dust, breathe dust and think dust.

T.E. LAWRENCE

It is the ultimate destiny of science to exterminate the human face.

THOMAS LOVE PEACOCK

There's nothing the British likes better than a bloke who comes from nowhere, makes it, and then gets clobbered.

MELVYN BRAGG *on Richard Burton*

People generally hate themselves. If it wasn't smack they'd hate themselves for eating carrots. You can bet on it.

KEITH RICHARDS

Prisons are places that make small criminals grow into big criminals.

HOWARD MARKS

As for that static ballroom mockery of dancing, a couple of swooning codfish clasped together in a hazy trance is nothing but an excuse for mutual masturbation.

CAITLIN THOMAS

Nostalgia is the graveyard of memory.

AUGUSTUS YOUNG

Tommy Cooper had a great rapport with himself.

RUSS ABBOTT

Dylan Thomas read f*** all because he was interested in f*** all bar himself.

KINGSLEY AMIS

DATING

I have to be careful dating. Is it me they're interested in or the image?

KATHERINE JENKINS

He'll never get a girlfriend if he keeps fouling up his breath with black pudding.

RICHARD NEWMAN *on Glyn Wise from* Big Brother 7

When I was dating Catherine [Zeta-Jones] first, every time I asked her to dinner I had to bring her whole family.

MICHAEL DOUGLAS

My courtship was spent leaning over the bottom halves of stable doors while Dick mucked out an endless row of stables.

MARY FRANCIS *on her famous jockey/author husband*

His first words to me were 'Has anybody ever told you you're a very pretty girl?' I said to myself, 'Oy gevaldt, here's the great lover, the great wit, the great intellectual of Wales, and he comes out with a line like that.'

LIZ TAYLOR *on Richard Burton's chat-up technique, or lack of it*

I'm a one-guy girl. One at a time, that is.

MANDY RICE-DAVIES

For my friends and me at 18, boys were the main topic of conversation. We wanted to know who got off with whom at which party, dissected crushes in minute detail and judged each other by who was on the Pill and who wasn't. Virginity was a hindrance and most of us had given it away for free by then.

ANNA SWAN

I look so ugly, the last time I was on a date the woman I was with asked me if we could skip straight to the cigarette.

CLEDWYN JONES

'Excuse me, Miss,' said the aspiring Lothario, 'I'm writing a phone book. Can I have your number?'

BRYN ELLIS

A scratch of bitchery in a woman is a necessity if she's to be noticed.

CAITLIN THOMAS

You know the old adage about treating a lady like a whore and a whore like a lady? Well for him it worked.

RAY MILLAND *on Clark Gable*

When I look into a girl's eyes I can tell just what she thinks of me. It's pretty depressing.

BOB HOPE

Most men secretly fancy large women. They love to sink themselves into softness, to sleep wrapped around curvy hips and swollen bellies, to rest their heads against ample bosoms. They keep this desire a dark secret, being seen out with coat hangers instead because fashion dictates it to be so.

DAWN FRENCH

Men are gluttons for punishment. They fight over women for the chance to fight *with* them.

VINCENT PRICE

The main difference between a Singles bar and a circus is that at a circus the clowns don't talk.

BRYN ELLIS

For a young girl to be named 'Wholesome' is perhaps the deadliest insult of all.

CAITLIN THOMAS

I've always wanted to place a personal ad no one would answer: 'Elderly, depressed, accident-prone junkie, likes Canadian food and Welsh music, seeking rich, well-built, over-sexed, female deaf mute in her late teens. Must be non-smoker.'

GEORGE CARLIN

DRINKING

Ryan Giggs and his brother Rhodri walk into a bar. Ryan says to the barman, 'I'll have what he's having'.

JOHN MCENTEE *on Giggs's alleged dalliance with Rhodri's wife*

I spent a third of my life drinking, a third asleep and a third with a hangover.

RICHARD BURTON

The only man who can beat a drinking Irishman is a drinking Welshman.

SHEILAH GRAHAM

Welsh livers and kidneys seem to be made of some metallic alloy quite unlike the rest of the human race.

BRIAN EVANS

Often he didn't know what day of the week it was. In company he was obnoxious and unreliable. He exploded daily. He was sometimes physically violent, often physically ill. There were many who thought he would beat Richard Burton, his *bête noir*, to an early grave.

QUENTIN FALK *on Anthony Hopkins during his drinking days*

I did stupid things like drive while drunk. In the mornings I would wonder, 'Did I kill somebody?' and check the front of the car.

HOPKINS *himself on the same time*

Beer rather than spirits is traditionally the drink that sends men to ruin in Wales. It is the reeking public bar and the 12 pints of flat, soapy beer on pay night that the chapels have inveighed against.

PAUL FERRIS

If you drink it straight down you can feel it going into each individual intestine.

RICHARD BURTON *on raicilla, the 180-proof distillate of the maguey plant*

An alcoholic is someone you don't like who drinks as much as you do.

DYLAN THOMAS

Jack London blamed his excessive drinking on the fact that no nurse was there to keep the liquor from his lips.

WALDO FRANK

Drunkenness is temporary suicide.

BERTRAND RUSSELL

If Snowdon is so wonderful, why is it there's not a pub on top?

GREN JONES

There are two reasons for drinking. One is when you are thirsty, to cure it. The other is when you are not, to prevent it. Prevention is better than cure.

THOMAS LOVE PEACOCK

I take my drinks neat. But sometimes I let my shirt-tail hang out a bit.

TOMMY COOPER

Whenever I'm asked what I want to drink to I always reply, 'To dawn'.

RACHEL ROBERTS

The main thing I do to keep fit is passing the vodka bottle.

KEITH RICHARDS

If there's one conjuring trick Tommy does successfully it's making a drink disappear.

GWEN COOPER *on her famous husband*

Drinking makes such fools of people and people are such fools to begin with. It compounds a felony.

ROBERT BENCHLEY

Some are born drunks, some achieve drunkenness, but Dylan Thomas liked to have drunkenness thrust upon him.

ANDREW SINCLAIR

An Irishman, an Englishman and a Welshmen walked into a pub. The barman said, 'Is this some kind of joke?'

BOB MONKHOUSE

Alcoholics Anonymous is like the Mafia. You don't get out of it and live.

ANTHONY HOPKINS

I've had 18 straight whiskeys. I think that's a record.

DYLAN THOMAS*'s reputed last words, probably apocryphal*

The first thing I do every morning after a binge is ask 'Who do I send flowers to?' I feel I'm bound to have behaved abominably the evening before.

RICHARD BURTON

I do not know who invented beer but I can say right off who have made the most fuss about it: the Welsh.

GWYN THOMAS

For a Welshman, life is a constant beer festival.

JOHN RICHARDS

The history of clandestine Sunday drinking has still to be written. There was a publican who laid a garden hose from his best-bitter pump to the front room of a neighbouring house.

TREVOR FISHLOCK

Coming from a nonconformist, teetotal Welsh background I was charmed by the guilt-free, amusing nature of drinking to excess as practised by the Irish. There was something so wonderfully un-English, un-Welsh and un-Scots about Dublin society where, if you needed to see your MP, you called around to his favourite bar, after hours, where he was busy getting drunk.

SIÂN PHILLIPS

If I die, let me die drinking in an inn.

WALTER MAP

All this drinking will be the urination of me.

RACHEL ROBERTS

I like the taste of beer, its live, white lather, its brass-bright depths, the sudden world through the wet brown walls of the glass.

DYLAN THOMAS

Some sheep farmers in mid Wales have formed a society of teetotallers. There's a clause in the rules that permits the use of alcohol at sheep-dipping time. One member keeps sheep at home for this purpose.

CHRISTIE DAVIES

Elizabeth Taylor didn't worry about another woman when she was married to Richard Burton. She worried about another man – Jack Daniels.

STANLEY BAKER

I woke up in France once and thought I was in Southampton.
CERYS MATHEWS

My players sank the white and now I'm going to sink the black.
IAN WOOSNAM *promising to lower some Guinness after his team won the 2006 Ryder Cup in Ireland*

I bet a man £20 I could cure my drinking problem. Now I've got a gambling problem as well.
TOMMY COOPER

Drink changed the environment around me. It made me feel like Humphrey Bogart or John Wayne. I remember seeing Sinatra on the stage in Las Vegas. He had a scotch and as he drank it he went 'Aahh!' and the whole audience went 'Aahh' with him. I knew that feeling but I couldn't stop with one. There wasn't enough booze in the world to satisfy me.
ANTHONY HOPKINS

Peter O'Toole was so drunk when he began to put a ring around my finger in *Becket* it was like a man trying to thread a needle wearing boxing gloves.
RICHARD BURTON

I hardly ever felt morning sickness because I was so used to hangovers.
CAITLIN THOMAS *on her pregnancy*

It only takes one drink to get me drunk. I'm not sure if it's the twelfth or thirteenth.
DYLAN THOMAS

Champagne for my real friends and real pain for my sham friends.
HUGH LLOYD-JONES

I love drunks. They're terrific until they throw up on you.

ANTHONY HOPKINS

They say 20 per cent of driving accidents are caused by drunken drivers. That must mean the other 80 per cent are caused by sober ones. If we all got drunk, therefore, there would be fewer accidents.

TOMMY COOPER

I have to think hard to name an interesting man who doesn't drink.

RICHARD BURTON

Pubs are more than tolerable places in which to be lonely.

JOHN OSBORNE

I was once told that a fan said he'd pay treble the price of a concert ticket if I sang Carmen's 'Habanera' while drunk.

KATHERINE JENKINS

I drank three bottles of vodka yesterday. It is not a good idea to drink so much. I shall miss all the marriages of my various children and they'll be angry because there'll be nobody around to make bad puns.

RICHARD BURTON

EDUCATION

Don't let school interfere with your education.

DAFYDD HUMPHRIES

I was a complete dud at school. Most of the teachers thought of me as a good-for-nothing.

STANLEY BAKER

I was educated not at Oxford but in the back seats of the Plaza in Swansea.

WYNFORD VAUGHAN-THOMAS

How long was Tom Jones in school? The ages of the 20 or so people I have spoken to that sat next to him range from 19 to 79. Has he actually left school yet? Also, would it be possible to have a look at an aerial photograph of Tom's house? When you consider that the same 20-odd people who sat by him in school used to live next door to him, then this suggests that Tom's house must look like a huge 20-sided 50p piece from above.

DAVID JANDRELL

Richard Burton was her university.

JOHN MORGAN *on Liz Taylor*

He attended or did not attend classes just as he pleased, recognising no timetable, sometimes strolling into or out of classes, or into or out of school, according to his whim. There was a transitional period during which no one was quite certain whether he was a pupil or not.

DAN JONES *on the schooldays of Dylan Thomas*

Audiences are the greatest teachers in the world.

RICHARD BURTON

A lot of the Welsh history we were taught at school was neither Welsh nor history.

DAFYDD CAMERON

The only coaching I ever received in my life was from a schoolmaster in Swansea. I was 12 at the time.

TREVOR FORD

I was sorely disappointed when I was interviewed at various teacher training institutions around the country. None of them were impressed by my ideas of teaching Ian McEwan's *The Cement Garden* [a novel about masturbation, murder and incest] to teenagers, or fostering their poetic spirits with Philip Larkin's 'They f★★★ you up/Your mum and dad'.

FRANCIS GILBERT

Do you know how I was educated? In 17 fights, nine lasting more than ten rounds, for a few shillings before I was 16. Then I went to the university of Joe Gess's boxing booth. At an early age I took honours in the great humanities.

TOMMY FARR

The best part of Sunday school was the Tree Top orange squash and Jammie Dodgers after prayers, which was either a reward or a bribe.

ANNA SWAN

Why am I the first Kinnock in a thousand generations to be able to get to university?

NEIL KINNOCK

While waiting for my 11-plus results I decided to fall ill. I was very bored with school and needed some attention and sympathy.

I had previously discovered that the mercury in a regular clinical thermometer could be flicked up almost as easily as it could be flicked down. So as long as no one was watching I could decide what temperature to be.

HOWARD MARKS

If you combined all three of their brains together I doubt whether they could solve a quadratic equation.

RICHARD BURTON *on the astronauts who landed on the moon in 1969*

It wasn't wise, I learned in school, to be too good at rugby. You might end up in the first 15 whose lot it was, if they persisted in losing, to be beaten by the Head until they started to win.

NIGEL JENKINS

University is a word that tastes like bad eggs in my mouth.

SAUNDERS LEWIS

Interviewer: 'What was life like at Chiswick Grammar?'
TOMMY COOPER: 'They were the happiest days of my life.'
Interviewer: 'Any particular reason?'
TOMMY COOPER: 'It was a girls' school.'

EGOTISM

I was the reason Elvis Presley started to play Vegas in the Seventies. He failed to crack it in the Fifties because he was too much of a rebel but he saw me do it and thought he'd try again.

TOM JONES

The two most beautiful things in the world are Ivor Novello's profile and my mind.

NOEL COWARD

I moved the whole world onto a 20-foot screen.

D.W. GRIFFITH, *the famous film director*

The megalomaniac differs from the narcissist in the fact that he wishes to be powerful rather than charming, and seeks to be feared rather than loved. To this type belong many lunatics, and most of the great men of history.

BERTRAND RUSSELL

I was the Marlon Brando of my generation.

BETTE DAVIS

Came out of the RAF Tuesday. Into a play Wednesday. Been a star ever since.

RICHARD BURTON

Autobiography is the height of egotism.

ROALD DAHL

What are the Welsh *for*? They are always so pleased with themselves.

ANNE ROBINSON

Churchill would make a drum out of the skin of his mother in order to sound his own praises.

DAVID LLOYD GEORGE

I can write anywhere. I can write in Florida. I can write in Cayman. I can write in aeroplanes. Mars? Why not.

DICK FRANCIS

I'd like to be reincarnated as myself.

GLYN WISE *from* Big Brother 7

Happy people are failures because they're on such good terms with themselves they don't give a damn.

AGATHA CHRISTIE

Bette Davis says, 'My name goes above the title. I am a star.' Yes she is a star, but is it worth playing all those demented old ladies to maintain that status?

MYRNA LOY

I'm my own greatest fan.

DAVID BOWIE

He was a cock who thought the sun had come up to hear him crow.

GEORGE ELIOT *on an acquaintance*

Rex Harrison was so pompous he expected women to open doors for him.

RACHEL ROBERTS

I'm not going to be modest anymore. I'm a movie star and it's lovely.

ANTHONY HOPKINS

The whole question of portraits is fraught with danger. As Kingman Brewster once told me: 'Remember this. If you say you like your portrait, people will say you are conceited. And if you say you don't like it, they will say you are even more conceited.'

GEORGE THOMAS

I don't find it at all amusing to paint stupid millionaires when I might be painting entirely for my own satisfaction.

AUGUSTUS JOHN

Just as at school he had to be 33rd at trigonometry, just as in America he had to be the drunkest man in the world, so in London in 1937 he could not simply be a poor poet: he had to be the most penniless of them all, ever.

CONSTANCE FITZGIBBON *on Dylan Thomas*

A little narcissism is necessary for an actress.

ELIZABETH HARRISON

I don't want to be a second-rate Burton. I want to be a first-rate Baker.

STANLEY BAKER

Acting is just people who used to be show-offs at school now showing off in front of other show-offs.

DAWN FRENCH

Unless you're going to be the greatest actor in the world, what's the point of getting into it?

RICHARD BURTON

If Barry John missed a penalty kick at goal in a tight international he would always come back muttering something about someone moving the posts.

GARETH EDWARDS

I was only 16 when I had a 'Best Of' compilation out. How mad is that?

CHARLOTTE CHURCH

Since when did a Welsh centre three-quarter wear a fake tan, spiked hair and silver boots? Did the legendary Bleddyn Williams take the field in full make-up? I think not.

HERMIONE EYRE *on Gavin Henson*

Gavin Henson is the vainest person in Wales. He's the type of man who would alternate his sleeping-side so he doesn't get wrinkles on one side of his face.

EMMA BLAIN

EISTEDDFODDAU

The eisteddfod is a week of merriment when those Welsh people who can speak the language lord it over those who can't.

GREN JONES

I've already got two chairs from eisteddfodau. I'm trying to exchange them for a sofa.

TUDUR DYLAN JONES

The eisteddfod is held in north Wales one year and south the next. This is to allow both north Walians and south Walians a chance to criticise the other's organisation of the event.

GREN JONES

A one-man eisteddfod of bruised sensibilities.

JAMES LAWTON *on Gavin Henson*

THE ENGLISH AND THE WELSH

To a Welshman a fence is for leaning on for a chat; to an Englishman it is to ensure privacy.

TREVOR FISHLOCK

No one seemed to understand that Wales was a completely separate country from England.

JOHN CHARLES's *perception of Italians after he joined Juventus*

Genuine English culture is rare in Wales, and rarest of all in the English-speaking areas.

RAYMOND GARLICK

If an Englishman enters a shop in Welsh-speaking parts of Wales, the locals are likely to switch promptly to speaking in Welsh. Thus the Englishman cannot be sure whether they are talking about him.

JOHN REDWOOD

Like you, we cake under the yoke of our Anglo-Saxon brothers. You, however, had much more sense than us in that you devoured as many of them as you could.

ALAN THOMAS, *the president of Welsh Rugby Union, welcoming the Fijian team in 1985*

Wales is so little different from England that it offers nothing to the speculation of the traveller.

SAMUEL JOHNSON

Wales has to bury its wars with England before it can really become Wales.

EDWARD THOMAS

Why do so many Welshmen marry Englishwomen? Because sheep can't fetch beer from the fridge.

MILES JEFFREYS

Most of the villains of Welsh history are, predictably, English. The most reviled is the Baron de Braose, who invited a number of Welsh chieftains to his castle and then murdered them at dinner. Murder was all right but the breach of hospitality was unforgivable.

JOHN RICHARDS

An Englishman trying to speak Welsh is like a man with a mouthful of scalding chips trying to answer the phone.

R.G. MAINWARING

Despite attempts to anglicise them, the Welsh have always remained foreigners to their English neighbours.

P. BERRESFORD ELLIS

The only time Wales gets a mention in London papers is when it carries the prefix, 'Princess of'.

MARION EAMES

The English and the Welsh are like an old married couple pulling the blankets off each other's back.

CHARLES WAY

I feel fearfully timid before the English. They conquered us and we remember it.

SAUNDERS LEWIS

For us this is the big game; little brother against big brother.

J.P.R. WILLIAMS *on Wales versus England in 1991*

I was out walking one day and a car stopped. A very English voice called out to a collier who happened to be passing, "Hey Dai, how do I get to Carmarthen?' The collier said, 'How did you know my name was Dai?' 'I guessed,' said the Englishman. 'Then you can guess your way to Carmarthen,' said the collier.

MAX BOYCE

On the English side of the Severn Bridge not many can name a Welsh writer other than Dylan Thomas.

ANNA SNOW

A Welsh geologist has claimed that Wales is bigger than England because of its hills. If it was rolled out flat it would be the bigger country of the two.

CHRISTIE DAVIES

The only English thing about me is my horror of showing emotion.

AUGUSTUS JOHN

Wales is always redefining itself so it won't wake up one day as England.

PAMELA PETRO

The Welsh seem no more dishonest than the English but they cheat you with a smile.

KINGSLEY AMIS

The Welsh feel sorry for the English in the same way that a social worker would make excuses for a criminal from a broken home: 'True, they did break into our country and steal everything they could get their hands on but the poor things are English after all.'

JOHN RICHARDS

We have a word in Welsh called *hwyl* which no English person can understand. It's an idiotic, marvellous, ridiculous longing for something.

RICHARD BURTON

What Welshmen have had to say in English is not Welsh literature.

WYN GRIFFITH

In England, the received idea of the Welsh has usually been that of a crowd of people who were folksy and quaint, mentally incomplete sometimes, and sometimes sharply devious – a little savage, probably dirty, somewhat servile, and with a comic way of speaking English. The Welsh, in popular imagination east of the dyke, were basically two-legged pit ponies who could sing, but you had to keep your eye on them or they would twist you.

TREVOR FISHLOCK

A Welshman free of both languages finds that the south [of Wales] is better pictured in English writing and the north in Welsh.

WYN GRIFFITH

Eddy was a tremendously tolerant person but he wouldn't put up with the Welsh. He always said, 'Surely there's enough English to go round'.

JOHN MORTIMER

After Dylan died, most Welsh people viewed me as little more than an English widow on holiday.

CAITLIN THOMAS

If two Englishmen are stranded on a desert island they form a queue. Two Welshmen would set up a committee.

HANNAH JONES

FAME

There aren't that many famous people in Wales. Have you seen the Welsh 'Guess Who'? The first question is always, 'Does she have a moustache?' If the answer is no, they say, 'It must be Bronwyn then'.

RHOD GILBERT

You can't frame applause, you can't place cheers on the mantelpiece and you can't plant a chuckle in a pot and expect it to raise laughs. All the average comic is left with at the end of his career are some yellowing newspaper cuttings, perhaps an LP or two and a couple of lines in *The Stage* obituary column.

HARRY SECOMBE

The famous are not always happy. They have to live not only with themselves but with our distorted picture of their brilliance, their wit, their beauty, their skill.

PAUL FERRIS

People regarded me differently after I became famous. If I didn't pay for something I was accused of being tight. If I did, they said I was a flash bastard. You couldn't win.

TERRY GRIFFITHS

It took me 15 years to discover I had no talent for writing but I couldn't give it up because by then I was too famous.

ROBERT BENCHLEY

There are no stars in Wales.

DAFYDD IWAN

One side of him scorned the glitter; the other went ahead and enjoyed it. It was as though he was the grit in his own oyster.

PAUL FERRIS *on Richard Burton*

I used to be an angel, now I'm the crazy chick. Where did plain ol' Charlotte go to?

CHARLOTTE CHURCH

In the days before my first cap I was flattered when camera crews followed me along the touchlines and reporters queued to talk to my Mam in her spotless kitchen, but there were to be times when I could have put everyone up against the wall and blown them up.

GARETH EDWARDS

If you spell 'star' backwards you get 'rats'.

RACHEL GRIFFITHS

My career is going swimmingly. The only problem is I'm not a swimmer.

DONALD HOUSTON

The main problem about being a famous actor is that everyone seems to think you know everything about everything. The plain fact of the matter is that actors know sod all about anything but acting. And most of them even know sod all about that.

HUGH GRIFFITH

Early acclaim won't harm a writer if he has enough cynicism not to believe it.

MARTIN AMIS

American women hunted Dylan in packs, conducting their courting with the ferocity of caged amazons. Nothing less than the evaporation of their prey would make them let go.

CAITLIN THOMAS

Fame means not being able to do anything, but doing it in front of the whole world.

SAUNDERS LEWIS

There's still a large part of me which is a working-class yob who wants to 'have it large'.

GREG CULLEN

Neither of us could handle the circus act surrounding our fame as it spiralled out of control.

BARRY JOHN *on himself and his friend George Best*

Jerry Springer said his show was garbage. Then they made an opera about it. That says it all about fame.

ESTHER RANTZEN

They treated me like a king in Italy. Youngsters would often come up and touch me if they saw me in the street, just to see if I was real.

IAN RUSH

I'm not a star yet but she's going to make me one. I'm going to use her, that no-talent Hollywood nothing.

RICHARD BURTON *to Eddie Fisher about Liz Taylor after he'd just met her*

Who would have thought a little girl from Tiger Bay would one day become a Dame?

SHIRLEY BASSEY

When Terry Griffiths won the world championship, he even knocked rugby off the back pages of the *Western Mail*.

PHIL DAVIES

It's better to be a has-been than a never-was.

JOHN OSBORNE

Fame, for Richard Burton, was a sweet poison one drinks first in eager sips, then in needful gulps. Then came the loathing of it and the profound ambivalence of its waning. For Burton it brought with it an unsettling sense of mortality. It became as necessary as air but it could never be grasped. With it he felt like a man attempting to empty the ocean with a fork. Its beginning, like everything, was its end.

GABRIEL BYRNE

FILMS AND FILMING

Your heart sank when you looked into those big doggy eyes.

RICHARD HARRIS *on Rachel Roberts*

It's impossible to direct yourself in a film.

STANLEY BAKER

I asked Dylan Thomas why he'd come to Hollywood. Very suddenly he said, 'To touch a starlet's tits'. I said, 'OK, but only one finger'.

SHELLEY WINTERS

Oh to play the man in the foreground instead of the blur in the background.

DESMOND LLEWELYN

The Welsh are the finest full-time actors in the world. We have no theatre but we do not need one. Life is a large enough stage for us.

RHYS DAVIES

James Dean is resurrected at regular intervals by cynical bosses and fans aren't quite convinced he's dead. Perhaps he's in Bolivia with Adolf Hitler. Elvis Presley has been seen recently in Memphis although he died in 1977. One star became president of the United States, so anything is possible.

HUGH LOUDON

I never played anything worthwhile apart from Q.

DESMOND LLEWELYN *on his famous Bond character*

He was tallish, thickish, with a face like a determined fist prepared to take the first blot but not the second. And if, for Christ's sake, you hurt certain aspects of his situation like his wife or his children, or even me, you were certain to be savagely destroyed.

RICHARD BURTON *on Stanley Baker*

Why did I leave *The Darling Buds of May*? There's only so much you can do with a piece of straw dangling out of your mouth.

CATHERINE ZETA-JONES

Cary Grant was more Celtic than British. He had the Welsh mood swings – duck or no dinner.

DAVID NIVEN

My hormones are just too way out of control to be dealing with this.

A heavily-pregnant **CATHERINE ZETA-JONES** *after being awarded an Oscar for her performance in* Chicago

They were the strolling players of the jet set.

MELVYN BRAGG *on Richard Burton and Liz Taylor*

The best part I ever played was the husband of Elizabeth Taylor.

RICHARD BURTON

I was the first actress who ever came out of the water looking wet.

BETTE DAVIS

Brad Pitt was recently released from hospital suffering from viral meningitis, which can influence tissue around the brain. The question is: Where has he been hiding that vital organ all these years?

BILLY MUIR

I never understood actors who had to be 'motivated'. My motivation was always my payslip.

STANLEY BAKER

We exponents of horror do much better than those Method actors. We make the unbelievable believable. More often than not, they make the believable unbelievable.

VINCENT PRICE

If Bob Hope was drowning he couldn't ad lib 'Help'.

HAL KANTOR

Richard Burton was the loneliest man I ever met.

MIKE NICHOLS, *who directed him in* Who's Afraid of Virginia Woolf?

They say actors learn more from their bad films than their good ones. In that case I must be very educated!

JONATHAN PRYCE

In *Snow Cake*, the snow almost becomes another character.

MARC EVANS

Richard Burton can charm the pants off anyone. Especially Elizabeth Taylor.

OSCAR LEVANT

Ray Milland didn't deserve an Oscar for *The Lost Weekend*. It was the film that was powerful, not the performance. In the same role W.C. Fields would have won.

JOHN HUSTON

A beauty contest for sheep has been put on to amaze the crowds at the Welsh film festival. If they'd really wanted to amaze people, they could just have put on a good Welsh film.

HAVE I GOT NEWS FOR YOU

They're doing things on the screen today that I wouldn't do on my honeymoon. Even if I could.

BOB HOPE

Mamie van Doren acted like Mr Ed the talking horse.

PAULA YATES

FOOT AND MOUTH DISEASE

Winning doesn't really matter as long as you win.

VINNIE JONES

We spoke about it for a while and out of it came the fact that he wouldn't speak about it.

TERRY VENABLES *on a conversation he had – or didn't have – with Middlesbrough chairman Steve Gibson about his future*

Young people, by definition, have their future before them.

NEIL KINNOCK

When I told President Bush I was from Wales, he said 'What state is that in?'

CHARLOTTE CHURCH

What's a walrus?

RACHEL RICE *from* Big Brother 9

Hard work is never easy.

JOHN TOSHACK

Last night I ordered an entire meal in French and even the waiter was surprised. It was a Chinese restaurant.

TOMMY COOPER

If history repeats itself I think we can expect the same thing again.

TERRY VENABLES

I went up the greasy pole of politics step by step.

MICHAEL HESELTINE

He's not unused to playing midfield but at the same time he's not used to playing there either.

EMLYN HUGHES

Führer is the proper name for him. He is a great and wonderful leader.

DAVID LLOYD GEORGE *on Hitler after meeting him in 1936*

Those are the sort of doors that get opened if you don't close them.

TERRY VENABLES

Are there any more great swimmers in the pipeline?

CLIFF MORGAN

They've got old shoulders on their heads.

J.P.R. WILLIAMS

Sadly, the immortal Jackie Milburn died recently.

CLIFF MORGAN

I've always been so frightfully proper.

MANDY RICE-DAVIES *after the Profumo scandal broke*

Richard Burton had a tremendous passion for the English language, especially the spoken and written word.

FRANK BOUGH

The past has been a big part of my life.

PAUL BURRELL

Graeme Souness went behind my back right in front of my face.

CRAIG BELLAMY

Djimi Traoré adapted to the English game by going out on loan to Lens last season.

IAN RUSH

Ian Rush is perfectly fit, apart from his physical fitness.

MIKE ENGLAND

Sometimes you open your mouth and it punches you straight between the eyes.

IAN RUSH

Charlotte more or less lives at my place now, which is probably why it's never looked as untidy.

GAVIN HENSON *in 2005*

There are two ways of getting the ball. One way is from your own players and that's the only way.

TERRY VENABLES

So, Woosie, you're from Wales. What part of Scotland is that?

American journalist to **IAN WOOSNAM** *during a 1987 press conference*

I'd like to go where the hand of man has never set foot.

TOMMY COOPER

What's a Liberal Democrat?

HELEN ADAMS *from* Big Brother 2

Before a storm in a teacup brews, nip it in the bud.

RUSSELL GRANT

People say I swear a lot. That's bollocks.

CHARLOTTE CHURCH

Is the jelly cooked?

HELEN ADAMS *during* Big Brother 2

Arsenal are streets ahead of everyone in the Premiership, and Man. United are up there with them.

CRAIG BELLAMY

Ryan Giggs did everything there but score or pass.

TOM TYRELL

Ian Rush unleashed his left foot and it hit the back of the net.

MIKE ENGLAND

Playing with wingers is more effective against European sides like Brazil than English sides like Wales.

RON GREENWOOD

You don't see as many red squirrels since they became extinct.

MICHAEL ASPEL

When you improvise, do you actually have to make it up?

PAULA YATES *once to an actor*

Jimmy Savile said he spent Christmas with Margaret Thatcher for ten years. That's a long Christmas.

IAN HISLOP

As Mr Hywel Morgan is indisposed and at present in hospital, we are pleased to say that he is progressing slowly.

WELSH PRESS

Russell Grant brings us the future before it happens.

MIKE MORRIS

I'll always remember 1995 as the year I found out *Star Trek* wasn't real.

DANIEL JOHNS

Football is a game. Tiddlywinks is a game. Cricket is like a cucumber sandwich. It seems to have been inspired to advance the values of sentry duty.

GRIFF RHYS JONES

Moving from Wales to Italy was like going to a different country.

IAN RUSH

FOOTBALL

I've just named the team that I would like to represent Wales in the next World Cup. Brazil.

BOBBY GOULD

For the first six months of my football apprenticeship I saw more paintbrushes than footballs.

IAN RUSH

I got a medal from Princess Di and a kiss from Sam Hammam. With no disrespect to either, I wish it had been the other way round.

VINNIE JONES *after receiving his FA Cup winner's award in 1988*

He's spent too much time being a father figure to players like me, which has meant he's had less time for other areas of his life.

RYAN GIGGS *on Alex Ferguson*

Goal-scorers were the heroes in Italy. Score the goal in a 1–0 win and you would have a caravan of cars driving up to your house hooting their horns in thanks. It was bad for sleep but very good for the image.

JOHN CHARLES

Ponderous as a carthorse and slow-witted as a football donkey, it's hardly Vinnie Jones's fault that such a clodhopper – sorry, former hod-carrier – has been able to wrangle a prosperous living from the professional game.

JEFF POWELL

Everything in football is advertising nowadays. It's only a matter of time before a player is fouled and he calls out to the stand, 'Have you had an accident at work yourself?'

LEE EVANS

Most of my goals were scored from the six-yard box. What some players forget is that it counts the same if it's a two-yard tap-in or a blockbuster from 30 yards.

IAN RUSH

Football isn't just about playing well. It's about making the other team play not so well.

ROY PAUL

Goalkeeping is about much more than saving shots.

NEVILLE SOUTHALL

You've got both ends of the spectrum at Newcastle. On the one hand there's Alan Shearer, who's rightly regarded as an ambassador for the game. On the other hand you have Craig Bellamy.

DEAN KIELY

If you win a game you're a genius. If you lose one you're worse than useless. There's no middle road.

JOHN TOSHACK

I don't take glove bags out with me that often now. It gives the opposition something to aim at.

NEVILLE SOUTHALL

Winning all the time is not necessarily good for a team.

JOHN TOSHACK

We know what we need to do now so I think we'll either win or lose.

IAN RUSH

If I had my way I'd ban substitutes from soccer. It's like a boxer with a cut eye or a broken fist. He either has to fight on or give in.

TREVOR FORD

Neville Southall was a big daft goalie. He had a sponsored car but he couldn't drive. And he once turned up at Wembley wearing his suit and a pair of flip-flops.

ANDY GRAY

I don't think we'll go down. But then again, the captain of the *Titanic* said the same thing.

NEVILLE SOUTHALL *on Everton's chances of avoiding relegation*

The image Mark Hughes conjures up is one that makes a caricaturist's pen convulse with joy: legs like tree trunks, neck muscles that put a pit bull terrier to shame, elbows flailing in the penalty box, and the guts of a kamikaze bungee jumper.

CEFIN CAMPBELL

Soccer is played with a ball, so why in heaven's name do clubs spend so much of the pre-season training lapping round the field?

TREVOR FORD

Whenever I see a sign outside a pub saying 'Live: England v. Croatia', I think: How are they going to fit them all in there?

LEE EVANS

If you're going to go over the top on me you better put me out of the game or I'll be coming back for you, either in five minutes or next season.

VINNIE JONES

So that's what you look like. I've played against you three times and all I've ever seen is your arse.

Soccer international **GRAHAM WILLIAMS** *to George Best after a bruising 1964 match*

Football is a funny game. Ron Davies scored 200 league goals in one season but the last I heard of him he was working somewhere on a building site.

GEORGE BEST *in 1982*

Ian Rush's hooter is so big he should have 'Long Vehicle' stencilled on the back of his head.

DANNY BAKER

Do Leeds fans hate Manchester United? Take a corner at Elland Road and you've got 15,000 horrible skinheads at their end yelling murder at you.

RYAN GIGGS

I used to meet Vinnie Jones in the old days for sausages, eggs, bacon, beans and a fried slice of bread before going off training. Now it's all pasta and vegetables.

DENNIS WISE

Ryan Giggs, the one with his eyes too close together, giving him the aspect of a village idiot.

MARIAN KEYES

Becks hasn't changed since I've known him. He's always been a flash Cockney git.

RYAN GIGGS

I read the Bible. The Old Testament was upsetting. Lots of wars and killing. God was much nastier than they'd told us in chapel. Was he American? St Paul was also a disappointment. But Jesus was great.

HOWARD MARKS

My father may not have believed in God but he believed in people.

STANLEY BAKER

If we Welshmen are the chosen race, how come God didn't give us webbed feet?

GREN JONES

There are Welshmen of my acquaintance who might opt for 'the other place' if God turned out to be an Englishman.

TREVOR FISHLOCK

I was told that the Chinese would bury me by the Western Lake and build a shrine to my memory. I have some slight regret that this did not happen, as I might have become a god, which would have been very chic for an atheist.

BERTRAND RUSSELL

In the US, golfers take as long to choose a club as a wife. Sometimes they make the wrong decision in each case.

DAI REES

I spent all day yesterday wading through streams and dropping hooks into deep water. That's the last time I'm going to waste playing golf.

TOMMY COOPER

Even a blind pig finds an acorn now and again.

IAN WOOSNAM *after coming out of a barren spell*

My girlfriend always thought Phillip Price was the bloke who played opposite Christopher Lee in the *Dracula* films.

LAWRENCE DONEGAN, *referring to Vincent Price*

Ian Woosnam says he's 5 feet 4½ inches but when he stands on the tee, he's nine feet tall.

BERNHARD LANGER

'How are you getting on with your new clubs?' asked the golfer when he walked into the bar and saw a friend of his. 'Fine,' replied the friend. 'They put 20 yards on to my slice.'

DAI REES

Now maybe they'll learn to spell my name right.

IAN WOOSNAM *after winning the Masters in 1991*

If Ian Woosnam ever grows up, he'll hit the ball 2,000 yards.

SANDY LYLE *after being beaten by Woosnam in the final of the 1987 World Matchplay Championship at Wentworth*

Golf is the only game where the worst player gets the best of it. He obtains more out of it as regards exercise and enjoyment. The good player gets worried over the slightest mistake whereas the poor player makes too many mistakes to worry about them.

DAVID LLOYD GEORGE

More players have fantasised about killing me than Jack the Ripper.

Course designer **ROBERT TRENT JONES** *who was infamous for his difficult lay-outs*

The only moment the Americans could have enjoyed during this year's Ryder Cup would have been watching champagne snot dribble slowly down from Ian Woosnam's nose at the victory celebrations.

RHODRI WINSTON *on Europe's decisive victory over the US in the 2006 event*

If you built the kind of course the pros would really like you would have dead flat greens, dead flat fairways, very little rough and very few traps. That kind of course wouldn't require an architect. You could order it from a Sears Roebuck catalogue.

ROBERT TRENT JONES

HEALTH

A nervous breakdown is the way we feel always.

DYLAN THOMAS

Assertive reassurance plus a placebo works well in mild affective disorders.

DANNIE ABSE

I said to the doctor, 'I have this ringing in my ears'. He said, 'Don't answer it'.

TOMMY COOPER

Good doctors are as rare as good actors.

RICHARD BURTON

Gareth calls the psychiatrist at a mental hospital and asks who's in room 24. 'Nobody,' comes the reply. 'Good,' says Gareth, 'I must have escaped'.

MILES JEFFREYS

If doctor and patient acknowledged each other as equals, the patient would not recover so quickly and the doctor would become ill.

DANNIE ABSE

Did you hear about the woman who went to her doctor complaining of nymphomania? He made her pay in advances.

OWEN MONEY

I'm sick of bloody doctors. The only pain I'd like them to remove is the pain in the arse they give me.

RICHARD BURTON

I go to a family doctor. He treats mine and I support his.

RHIANNON REES

Richard Burton was so vigorous and healthy as Hamlet, I can positively say that it was the only version of the play I ever saw where one felt sorry for Claudius.

OSCAR LEVANT

I stuffed their mouths with gold.

ANEURIN BEVAN *on how he dealt with consultants when establishing the National Health Service*

I have a problem with the term 'stroke'. It's such a nice word for such a terrible condition. It's like saying, 'How's Tim?' and getting the answer, 'Haven't you heard? It's awful. He's had a cuddle.'

KEITH BARRET

Be careful about lending money. It has medical side-effects. It can lead to amnesia.

ROY NOBLE

I have to ruin my health because I feel so preposterously well.

DYLAN THOMAS

I asked a waiter if he had frog's legs. He said, 'No, it's the rheumatism that makes me walk like this.'

HARRY SECOMBE

I suppose you could live on boiled eggs if the chips were down.

RICHARD BURTON

I went to the doctor last week because I had a cucumber stuck in one ear, a carrot in the other and two peas up my nose. I asked him what was the matter with me. 'I don't think you're eating properly,' he told me.

TOMMY COOPER

I always get an attack of piles on the third week of shooting.

RICHARD BURTON

Dylan kept saying he would die before me and I would be a flighty widow dancing on his grave. And I laughed, completely unmoved. For all the impression it made on me, he might as well have been talking to an elephant.

CAITLIN THOMAS

I hurt my back the other day. I was playing piggyback with my six-year-old nephew and I fell off.

TOMMY COOPER

Richard Burton had an acne-rough complexion you could scratch a match on.

TRUMAN CAPOTE

HOSTILITY

Why don't you f★★★ off back to Italy!

NEVILLE SOUTHALL *to Ian Rush after Rush scored a hat-trick against him in his testimonial match shortly after leaving Juventus*

Tony Richardson brutalises actors. How the hell is he going to direct his films if one day they all walk off the set?

ANTHONY HOPKINS

I hate weak things. When the hippies came along I wanted to hit anyone with love beads.

DAVID BOWIE

The stairs have disappeared. She's chopped them up with her bare hands.

LENNY HENRY *joking about the alleged PMT of his ex-wife Dawn French*

It's no fun being at loggerheads with me. I can drain the energy out of anyone that fights with me. I don't enjoy it but I can be a hard f★★★er.

KEITH RICHARDS

One of his favourite sports was to go out on the road and attack passing cars with his bare fists.

ELIZABETH HARRISON *on Richard Harris*

Sometimes I think I would have been a better player with a bit of the devil in me. When I look back on the players who gave me a bashing I kind of regret not bashing them back.

JOHN CHARLES

Roy Keane could start a fight in an empty room.

RYAN GIGGS

If the shoulder charge is banned from soccer, soccer will die. Just as well take the hops from beer or the salt and vinegar from the late night bag of fish and chips.

TREVOR FORD

Pol Pot killed 1.7 million Cambodians and died under house arrest. Well done. Stalin killed many millions also, and died in his bed aged 72. Well done again. The reason we let them get away with it is that they killed their own people. Hitler's problem was that he killed people next door, and we can't stand for that, can we?

EDDIE IZZARD

One of my favourite hobbies is dancing on the graves of the people who told me I'd never make it.

ANTHONY HOPKINS

When I arrived at Richard Harris' door once, I was greeted by his wife Elizabeth with the words, 'Hello Malachy, when are you leaving?'

MALACHY MCCOURT

A lot of warm vulgarity is incomparably preferable to a little bit of pinched niceness.

CAITLIN THOMAS

The fact that I'm unemployed helps to add to my natural hatred of Wales.

DYLAN THOMAS

I had a ploughman's lunch the other day. He wasn't half mad.

TOMMY COOPER

IMAGE

Goalkeepers get a bad rap. It goes back to your schooldays when he was the last person to be picked because he was regarded as the worst player on the pitch.

NEVILLE SOUTHALL

Anthony Hopkins' favourite novel is *The Great Gatsby* and one can see why – like Jay Gatsby he is someone who has concocted the externals of a life but not the inner workings. He has succeeded in everything he set out to do except somehow be himself.

LYNN BARBER

Richard Burton continues to portray himself as an academic *manqué* – Faust, in other words, the scholar who sold his soul to the devil. But he never makes it clear whether that devil is Elizabeth Taylor or the movies.

BRENDA MADDOX

Elizabeth Taylor was as pinned to her public stardom as a trapped suburban housewife was to her kitchen.

MELVYN BRAGG

The role of the drunken Welsh poet with the fag in the corner of the mouth and the dirty raincoat and polo sweater sometimes lasted for a week or more with him, but not longer.

DONALD TAYLOR *on Dylan Thomas*

Humphrey Bogart may have seemed tough but he came from a posh family. I had to give him lessons on how to look poor.

RICHARD BURTON

The Wales of leeks, daffodils, and look-you-know-boyo rugby supporters' singing Max Boyce songs in three-part harmony while phoning Mam to tell her they'll be home for tea and Welsh cakes has gone. The Wales I know is bilingual, multicultural, pro-European, messed-up, screwed-up, and ludicrously misrepresented in the British press.

EDWARD THOMAS

You can shove the 'Boozie Woosie' stuff down the bog. I didn't get to number one in the world by swilling beer.

IAN WOOSNAM *on his drinking image*

John Cale is a pussycat in panther's clothing.

BETSEY JOHNSON

I'm half-British and half-American. My passport has an eagle with a teabag on its beak.

BOB HOPE

I've been called everything from a Roman Catholic to a literary Marx brother.

DYLAN THOMAS

One journalist described me as a 'wide-eyed Bambi on speed'.

KATHERINE JENKINS

INSULTS

I hate every living person, with the exception of a Mrs McCarthy who lives in Chelsea.

DYLAN THOMAS

When Dannii Minogue was a child, a dingo ran off with her talent.

MARK LAMARR

That insolent little ruffian, that crapulous lout. When he quitted a sofa, he left behind him a smear.

NORMAN CAMERON *on Dylan Thomas*

A sink-estate yob on a one-way ticket to Alcoholics Anonymous.

CAROLE MALONE *on Charlotte Church*

Environmentalists tell us every day that areas the size of Wales are destroyed. Why is it never Wales?

JIMMY CARR

Not so much *Hamlet* as Richard Burton playing Richard Burton playing *Hamlet*.

GRAHAM JENKINS *on his famous brother in Shakespeare's most famous play*

I used to be pleased when an American friend wrote, 'Thank you for your good letter.' Later, though, several other American correspondents thanked me for my good letters and gradually I realised that they no more meant it than I did when I asked them to convey my greetings to their 'good' ladies, whom I secretly suspected may well have been bitches or harlots.

DANNIE ABSE

The emotional appeal in Auden wouldn't raise a corresponding emotion in a tick.

DYLAN THOMAS

Volatile, dominant, highly energised, svelte, acerbic and coruscating are all words that Terry Jones uses with uncertainty.

JOHN CLEESE

I was cleaning out the attic the other day with the wife. Filthy, dirty and covered in cobwebs. But she's good with the kids.

TOMMY COOPER

Richard Church is a cliché-ridden humbug and pie-fingering hack.

DYLAN THOMAS

Don't you know that you're depriving a village somewhere of an idiot?

RHOD GILBERT *to a heckler at one of his shows*

The museum in Swansea should have been in a museum.

DYLAN THOMAS

The paparazzi have got out of hand. If they could sell them, they'd take pictures of one urinating.

RICHARD BURTON

Harri Webb is the Max Boyce of Welsh literature.

MARION ELLIS

Gavin Henson's hair could give a small dog a run for its money. He gets through tins of Dax Wave and Groom at the rate old-fashioned rugby players sank beer.

TANYA ALDRED

The worst club I ever played was in Queensferry. The toilets were cleaner than the dressing room.

ROY 'CHUBBY' BROWN

No Welsh writer can hunt his bread and butter in Wales unless he tugs his forelock to the *Western Mail*, enters public houses by the back door, and reads Caradoc Evans only when alone, and by candlelight.

DYLAN THOMAS

Cedric Hardwicke had all the personality of an old tortoise hunting for lettuce.

RACHEL ROBERTS

Taffy was a Welshman, Taffy was a thief. That was a pretty good accurate description of Dylan.

CAITLIN THOMAS

Janet Street-Porter should have her vocal chords forcibly removed.

MITCHELL SYMONS

LANGUAGE

Welsh struggles like a hothouse flower in the chill of its own soil.
PAMELA PETRO

To the ordinary Englishman, the greatest of all strangenesses is a strange language in a familiar country.
WYN GRIFFITH

If something is in Welsh on television it has to be first-class because no one is going to put up with rubbish out of loyalty if he can switch over and get something better in English.
RYAN DAVIES

In Wales all can be forgiven except being serious about the language.
SAUNDERS LEWIS

I would like Anglo-Welsh writers to see themselves first as Welshmen. The only English thing about an Anglo-Welsh writer ought to be his language.
GLYN JONES

The main function of Welsh writers is to write about the language struggle.
ANGHARAD TOMOS

I am not a Welsh writer because I do not write in the language the English language calls Welsh.
DIC EDWARDS

My father and mother were Welsh-speaking, yet I did not exchange a word in that language with them. The death of Welsh ran through our family of 12 like a geological fault.
GWYN THOMAS

I believe in applying eugenics to language because the offspring of decently married words is a very sweet and whimsical girl called poetry and I don't think it is fair to her to be born into this world with a hideous deformity for all the beastly staring critics to point and sneer at.

SAUNDERS LEWIS

Her father had what the Welsh call 'hwyl', a very evocative style of preaching. It explains where she got her power, though not her subtlety.

RONNIE CASS *on Rachel Roberts*

Welsh is like Silly Putty. You can stretch it and twist it and mould it into any number of shapes and it's still Welsh – which is both a boon and an anxiety for learners.

PAMELA PETRO

Accents? I can do Irish, Welsh, Manchester, Liverpool, Birmingham, Cockney and New York Jewish lesbian.

JULIE WALTERS

I am as thrilled by the English language as I am by a lovely woman green as dreams or deep as death.

RICHARD BURTON

What's a womb in Welsh? Here lies the problem. Apparently it's 'croth', but I thought that was something biblical that Mary had. Sex is such an 'Ych a Fi' disgraceful thing; we couldn't possibly face each other over cornflakes if we did it in our mother tongue.

SIÂN MELANGELL DAFYDD

Blessed is the man who, having nothing to say, abstains from giving wordy evidence of the fact.

GEORGE ELIOT

Welsh is a dead language. Petrol pump is 'pwmp petrol'. Atomic bomb is 'bom atomig'. A tin of salmon is 'tun o samwn'. And what is the Welsh word for bingo? Ha, ha.

T. GLYNNE DAVIES

Although Welsh sounds mellifluent [*sic*] to me, some people tell me that to their mind it's gibberish: 'The Welsh and their yuck talk.' 'It's like belching.' 'The wogs begin at Chepstow.' And so on.

TREVOR FISHLOCK

I could recite curses fluently long before I could stumble through the words of 'Abide with Me'.

TOMMY FARR

Let English be the language of commerce and Welsh the language of religion.

THOMAS GEE

The majority of Welsh speakers will not ask for forms and documents in their own language. It will take two generations to teach the Welsh-speaking Welsh to use it without shame or fear.

ISLWYN ELIS

Gerard Manley Hopkins' ignorance of Welsh actually improved his poetry. The words he made up enhanced his rhythms.

NORMAN WHITE

Alan Rickman's wonderfully suggestive drawl alone seems to wire some of his fans up to the National Grid.

MAUREEN PATON

Speech may be barren but it is ridiculous to suppose that silence is always brooding on a nest full of eggs.

GEORGE ELIOT

There is a great difference between a Welsh accent and a Welsh intonation.

DAN JONES

I always called a spade a spade until the night I fell over one in the dark.

HARRY SECOMBE

Richard Burton once told me he even dreamt in Welsh.

ROSEMARY KINGSLAND

Plaid Cymru's policy for Welsh smallholdings: 'Five acres and a Welsh-speaking cow.'

CHRISTIE DAVIES

Anyone who speaks any language other than Welsh is not Welsh.

WELSH MIRROR

Until the history and culture of Wales find some place in UK schools, the Welsh language will remain at best a rumour, at worst a secret.

ROBERT MINHINNICK

Afrikaans sounds like Welsh with emphysema.

A.A. GILL

Why does Charlotte Church swear so much? Is it to remind us she's Welsh?

MICHAEL PARKINSON

I went to Europe once. They talk funny there. It's a bit like Wales.

IAN BOUMPHREY

I used to be dyslexic but I'm KO now.

TOMMY COOPER

'Taxi' in Welsh is 'Tacsi', written that way for the benefit of Welsh people who've never seen an 'X' before.

KINGSLEY AMIS

A lot of people make fun of my accent. A friend of mine said, 'I can never do the Welsh accent. If I try, it comes out Pakistani.' I said, 'Well you've got to try harder to master it... Ahmed.'

MARK WATSON

LITERATURE

Literature is basically the great freemasonry of loneliness.
GWYN THOMAS

All autobiography is a form of suicide.
DANNIE ABSE

I'm not much good at writing letters. I can't strike the happy medium between trying to be funny, not trying to be funny, and trying not to be funny.
DYLAN THOMAS

Writing is a tricky business and writing about writing is even trickier.
EMYR HUMPHREYS

When you are creating, it takes up all of you. Genius is selfish.
CAITLIN THOMAS

The best time for planning a book is while you're doing the dishes.
AGATHA CHRISTIE

I wish Charlotte Bronte's characters would talk a little less like the heroes and heroines of police reports.
GEORGE ELIOT

Harri Webb was aware that if you want to tell people the truth you better make them laugh or they'll kill you.
NIGEL JENKINS

The easiest kinds of characters to write are lonely ones because a writer is usually lonely while he's writing.
DICK FRANCIS

The greatest obstacle to professional writing is the necessity of changing a typewriter ribbon.

ROBERT BENCHLEY

I despise all those phoney Welsh novels and stories about the wry rhetorical wisdom of poetic miners and the boring myths about the wonder and glory of life in the Valley towns – all those canonisations of literary deadbeats, charlatans and flops.

KINGSLEY AMIS

I can't write poetry in Welsh, only prose.

R.S. THOMAS

A manifesto usually intimidates a writer and is meaningless after a few weeks.

IDRIS DAVIES

'Literature.' Dylan had a special way of uttering this word. He didn't spit it out or say it with a snarl. It was as if he had suddenly bitten into a sloe or a stick of green rhubarb.

DAN JONES *on Dylan Thomas*

Sometimes I think the flaws in my work are more interesting than the things I'm good at.

EDWARD THOMAS

Sometimes Dylan made his poems completely unintelligible. He'd joke afterwards that he couldn't understand them himself.

CAITLIN THOMAS

Dylan Thomas was a monster. You wouldn't take him home to your mother even if you were certain she was out.

CON HOULIHAN

I live from poem to mouth and both suffer.

DYLAN THOMAS

LOOKS

I like women who look like women. I hated grunge. No one is more of a feminist than me but you shouldn't look like you don't give a shit.

CATHERINE ZETA-JONES

He told me once that he used to rub his nose with his fist before the mirror every morning until it shone satisfactorily, as a housewife might polish her doorknob.

CONSTANCE FITZGIBBON *on Dylan Thomas*

I don't want to end up like some British stars in Hollywood who sit around the pool all day until their teeth fall out. Then they get capped ones and face jobs and end up in TV series.

ANTHONY HOPKINS

Bill Buckley's face looks like a triumph of plastic surgery after a bad car accident.

RICHARD BURTON *on the American TV talk show host*

Being short made me feel an underdog when I was a boy. I still have a sense that I need to work twice as hard as anyone else to beat the odds.

IAN WOOSNAM

Big noses run in my family.

TOMMY COOPER

I will never forget the first time I clapped eyes on Ian Rush. I think it was the combination of that eyebrow-pencil moustache and the corduroy drainpipes that made him such an unforgettable sight.

KENNY DALGLISH

Dorothy Kilgallen had no chin, Louella Parsons had no neck, and Hedda Hopper had to wear strange hats to stand out in a crowd. I don't believe most of the men columnists were failed actors but most of the women gossips took out their frustrations on the beautiful actresses who became stars. They wrote with green ink.

RAY MILLAND

My bottom is so big it has its own gravitational field.

CAROL VORDERMAN

A mutant begot by a heavyweight boxer in a car crash in Baghdad.

CLIVE JAMES *on Tommy Cooper*

Not only did I have unfashionable beige hair, horrible National Health pink spectacles, big sticking-out front teeth and the longest, thinnest legs at school, I also had a flat chest.

JANET STREET-PORTER

I always admired Katharine Hepburn's cheekbones more than her films.

BETTE DAVIS

Trinny Woodall is an anorexic transvestite.

CAROL VORDERMAN

I've got cankles. That's when your calves run down to your ankles

CHARLOTTE CHURCH

A beautiful doughnut covered in paint.

ALAN WILLIAMS *on Liz Taylor at her fortieth birthday party*

It's a plastic surgeon I'm wanting.

TOMMY FARR *after being carved up by Joe Louis in his famous 1937 fight with the boxing legend*

Howard Marks makes Peter Pan look like a geriatric with sleeping sickness.

LOADED *magazine*

Mark Hughes is playing better and better, even if he's going grey and starting to look like a pigeon.

GIANLUCA VIALLI *in 1997*

The Lord likes common-looking people. That is why he made so many of them.

ABRAHAM LINCOLN

If I had a face like Elizabeth Taylor I'd never have won two Oscars.

BETTE DAVIS

I was a bit disillusioned when Ingrid Bergman left her husband and daughter for Roberto Rossellini in 1949. Not because she left her husband and daughter but because Rossellini looked like a heavy from a B-feature.

HUGH LOUDON

When I was born my mother said I looked like a frog.

CATHERINE ZETA-JONES

Phyllis Diller has had so many facelifts there's nothing left in her shoes.

BOB HOPE

His face was his misfortune. Ivor was tripped up by his beauty.

PHYLLIS BOTTOME *on Ivor Novello*

When one has got used to wearing brilliant shirts and being stared at, all feeling of glamour fades away – but the mud, sweat and bumps are left.

DICK FRANCIS *on the gritty reality of being a jockey*

I think you'd better come at once, doctor. I don't like the look of my wife.

JOHN EDWARDS *quoting an unfortunate turn of phrase used by an acquaintance on the phone*

She is as beautiful as an erotic dream, tall and extremely large bosomed. Tremendously long legs. They go up to her shoulders. And beautiful brown eyes set in a vulpine, almost satanic face.

RICHARD BURTON *on Liz Taylor*

I've always pictured Ian Woosnam in a medallion with a 'Kiss Me Quick' hat on.

TOM HUMPHRIES

A woman says to her doctor: 'I've got a bad back.' The doctor says, 'It's old age'. The woman says she wants a second opinion. The doctor says, 'OK, you're ugly as well'.

TOMMY COOPER

There's nothing worse than reading a script and your character gets introduced with the words 'A beautiful woman walks in'. You think: Oh God that means two and a half hours in make-up.

CATHERINE ZETA-JONES

When I won the Rear of the Year Award there were more photographers at the photo call than at any other one I've ever done.

CHARLOTTE CHURCH

Her tits are apocalyptic. They could topple empires.

RICHARD BURTON *on Liz Taylor*

The Queen looks like Helen Mirren.

MICHAEL SHEEN

Eighty-three per cent of Britons say they forgive Princess Di for her infidelity. Apparently the other 17 per cent haven't gotten a good look at Prince Charles.

CONAN O'BRIEN

LOVE

'Love your neighbour' isn't merely sound Christianity; it's good business too.

DAVID LLOYD GEORGE

To fear love is to fear life and those who fear life are already three parts dead.

BERTRAND RUSSELL

Love is always in the mood for believing in miracles.

JOHN COWPER POWYS

I was in love once. It was an awful experience. It rotted me. It was a disease.

DAVID BOWIE *in 1976*

Most Welshmen love Wales more than most Englishmen love England.

TREVOR FISHLOCK

We're in danger of loving ourselves to death.

JOHN PRESCOTT *on the Labour Party in 1994*

All American films boil down to one thing: 'I love you, Dad.'

IAN HISLOP

Mary and I smiled at each other and to my astonishment, before we had even spoken, I found myself thinking, 'This is my wife'. I had never believed in love at first sight and it still seems to be an unreasonable way of choosing a companion for life but there it was in a flash between us, our future pledged in a glance.

DICK FRANCIS *upon first meeting the woman he was to marry*

Of all forms of caution, caution in love is perhaps the most fatal to true happiness.

BERTRAND RUSSELL

It is quite natural for an actor to fall in love with his leading lady during a play or film. It's harmless because he can always walk away.

RICHARD BURTON, *who couldn't*

Instead of having to pretend that I loved him I had to pretend that I was pretending I did and that is not half so easy.

CAITLIN THOMAS *on a paramour*

I love this place. It's what Catholic Wales was like before Nonconformism laid its hand on it.

SIÂN PHILLIPS *on County Kerry in Ireland*

I have been paid fabulous sums to frolic with and make bogus love to the most beautiful women in the world.

RAY MILLAND

Monty, Elizabeth likes me but she loves you.

RICHARD BURTON *to Montgomery Clift about his future wife*

Some people say that the Welsh have a love-hate relationship with the English. They are, in fact, 100 per cent wrong. For a start, there's precious little love involved.

JOHN RICHARDS

Towards the apathetic I am apathetic. I don't bother to attack Harry John Doe Jones because he is not worth my attention but show me a loved one and the bludgeon and sabre are out and my name is Fang.

RICHARD BURTON

Love is nurtured by kicking and biting.

OLD WELSH SAYING

Dylan Thomas's emotional life would suggest that no man was ever more adept at killing what he loved.

JOHN MALCOLM BRINNIN

Michael Wilding is in love with himself but he isn't sure if it's reciprocated.

RICHARD BURTON

MARRIAGE

For my wedding I'm trying to get into shape. The shape I picked is a triangle.

DAWN FRENCH

Throughout our marriage my wife has always stood by me. She has to. We've only got one chair.

TOMMY COOPER

I have some very dear great-aunts who informed me that if I insisted on marrying a Catholic in a Catholic church I would be cut out of their wills on the spot. Since it came as a surprise to me that I was ever in them, my expectations of becoming an heiress were short-lived.

ELIZABETH HARRISON *on her decision to marry Richard Harris*

The fact that husbands don't live as long as wives can be seen as nature trying to make up for the inequality of sexism. Some widows are bereaved but many are simply relieved.

RACHEL ROBERTS

When my wife starts to nag me I feel like taking the dog out for a walk. Even though I don't have a dog.

LEE EVANS

I was very devoted to Rex Harrison before we were married and after we were divorced. It was that little bit in between which proved difficult.

ELIZABETH HARRISON

My wedding day went like these things do: full of anxious moments interspersed with black comedy.

JANET STREET-PORTER

Marriage is the tomb of friendship.

RICHARD BURTON

The nature of my job has meant that I have been away for between 30 and 35 weeks of each year. It's a reality my wife has accepted ever since that difficult moment when I told her we wouldn't be able to go on honeymoon because I was already committed to playing a tournament starting in Indonesia on the Thursday after our wedding.

IAN WOOSNAM

Better the lumpy mattress of marriage than the feather bed of sin.

CARADOC EVANS

I was 22 when I married. In those days it was the only way you could have a sex life.

ANNE COLLEDGE *on the Fifties in north Wales*

A real Welshman will always celebrate his wedding anniversary – sometimes even with his wife.

GREN JONES

If you ever asked her to sort out a problem involving Bernard, it was always, 'My husband right or wrong.'

FRANCIS THOMAS *on Laura Ashley*

The most difficult year of marriage is the one you're in.

FRANKLIN P. JONES

Liz Taylor and Richard Burton split up but they didn't like it and remarried. But they didn't like that either so they split up again. This could have gone on until they both died.

JO BRAND

Zsa Zsa Gabor got married as a one-off but it was so successful she turned it into a series.

BOB HOPE

I met my wife at the travel bureau. She was looking for a vacation and I was the last resort.

TOMMY COOPER

Why is it so easy to get hold of other men's wives and not get one of your own?

W.H. DAVIES

Richard Burton is alleged to have broken up seven marriages during his 12 years in Hollywood.

SAM KASHNER

Just because divorce was beyond your parents doesn't mean that it's beyond you. It won't be easy. You'll have to dig deep inside your heart for inspiration.

KEITH BARRET

Lenny [Henry] and myself renewed our wedding vows in Las Vegas. I laughed so much I wet my knickers. It makes a mockery of everything you think about marriage. Plastic flowers, Velcro-fastened dresses and a preacher who had to look at a prompt sheet to remember your name.

DAWN FRENCH

An archaeologist is the best husband any woman can have. The older she gets, the more interested he is in her.

AGATHA CHRISTIE

I've been married six months. She looks like a million dollars but only knows 120 words and she's only got two ideas in her head. The other one's hats.

ERIC LINKLATER

Would I consider remarriage? Yes, if I found a man who had $15 million, would sign over half of it to me before becoming my husband, and guarantee he'd be dead within a year.

BETTE DAVIS

After a while marriage is a sibling relationship marked by occasional, rather regrettable, episodes of incest.

MARTIN AMIS

Aristotle maintained that women have fewer teeth than men. Although he was twice married it never occurred to him to verify this statement by examining his wives' mouths.

BERTRAND RUSSELL

My grandfather had been married twice, a state which in Wales is looked upon rather like leprosy.

RAY MILLAND

A Welsh perfectionist is a man who, if he was married to Catherine Zeta-Jones, would expect her to be able to cook.

DAFYDD ELLIS

The bottle is like a second wife to Richard Burton – and who wants to break up a happy marriage?

KENNETH TYNAN

Marriage is a lottery but if you lose you can't tear up the ticket.

STAN STENNETT

The best part of marriage is the arguments.

ROALD DAHL

Divorce, divorce, divorce. You say it's an ending, I say it's a fresh start. Is the glass half full or half empty? If you're a man who's recently divorced the chances are you don't have any glasses left.

KEITH BARRET

Spanish has the same word for handcuffs and wives. Go figure.

HOWARD MARKS

The marriage between Richard Burton and Liz Taylor was about as tranquil as a bad gear change in a ten-foot lorry.

DONALD ZEC

Graffiti spotted in a Llangollen pub at Eisteddfod time: 'Marriage is like playing a Stradivarius – beautiful music with strings attached.'

BILL SHIPTON

My first husband and I lived happily never after.

BETTE DAVIS

A Hollywood marriage is one where both parties agree to be faithful until after the honeymoon.

DAVID MCCALLUM

Throughout the whole of our marriage Dylan never spent a single evening at home.

CAITLIN THOMAS

My wedding to Sally Hay was the only one at which I was sober.

RICHARD BURTON

I remember a Welsh actor saying, 'Actors need wives but they should never get married.'

VINCENT DOWLING

Very few men are generous enough to accept success in their wives.

SHIRLEY BASSEY

Welshmen prize their women so highly that they put a picture of their mother-in-law on the national flag.

LES DAWSON *on the dragon symbol*

The press gets my relationship with Charlotte wrong. There was one picture of us sitting on sun-loungers on the beach and because we were a few yards apart it was claimed we weren't speaking, and on the point of splitting up. The truth was that Charlotte had moved into the shade because she was hot.

GAVIN HENSON

After Lizzie Taylor married Dick Burton they stayed in bed for three years.

GROUCHO MARX

Why did I marry Elizabeth twice? Because the murderer always returns to the scene of the crime.

RICHARD BURTON

If I hadn't got married I'd probably be at Her Majesty's pleasure somewhere doing bird.

VINNIE JONES

The only reason to get married now is inheritance tax.

JONATHAN PRYCE

For marriage to be a success, every woman and every man should have her and his own bathroom. The End.

CATHERINE ZETA-JONES

MEN AND WOMEN

I see women's role in life in the light of sweetness. Men should be the hunters. Women are keepers of the hunters.

LAURA ASHLEY

Men, I learned, behaved like children when they had drink taken. 'In vino' was never 'veritas'. Drunken talk made no sense. Women shrugged tolerantly and loftily in the face of masculine stupidity. Clever women never nagged. Clever women dodged the flying cutlery and went away where they could get some peaceful sleep and never in the morning referred to the excesses of the night before.

SIÂN PHILLIPS

The history of my relationship with women is largely one of immoral curiosity.

RICHARD BOOTH

All men are swine. I grew up in a world where no one was ever faithful.

CAITLIN THOMAS

There are a lot of women who live with pot-bellied pigs.

CATHERINE ZETA-JONES

He kissed her once by the pigsty when she wasn't looking and never kissed her again although she was looking all the time.

DYLAN THOMAS

It suits Richard Burton to have Liz Taylor fat – like a man who is always making his wife pregnant so she'll never have the chance to look at another man.

SHEILAH GRAHAM

It's still scary being a woman, even in 2006. There are parts of Tennessee where they're told what colour shoes to wear at particular times of the year.

CERYS MATHEWS

Augustus John's portraits of men were usually better than his of women. I think this was probably because he was trying to woo the women at the same time. He would give them necks a yard long and huge eyes in order to flatter them, seducing them with paint before flinging them onto his couch.

CAITLIN THOMAS

For my father it seems there were only good girls and bad girls. Perhaps the wordsmith in him saw that lust is an anagram of slut.

ANNA SWAN

I hardly ever meet any Bond girls because I do all my scenes with Bond. It's very sad.

DESMOND LLEWELYN, *aka 'Q' in the James Bond movies*

There's only one woman I know who failed to be ensnared by the legendary charm of Richard Burton – Marie Dressler. She died before he met her.

RAYMOND MASSEY

Even nowadays a man can't step up and kill a woman without feeling just a little bit unchivalrous.

ROBERT BENCHLEY

I would prefer to gnaw my arm off than get into a confrontation with her.

LENNY HENRY *on his ex-wife Dawn French*

Men stay in pubs for one of two reasons: (a) They don't have a wife to go home to, and (b) They *do* have a wife to go home to.

MARGIAD PRYCE

Dylan insisted women were a spewing mass of generalisations and clichés only fit for the bed or the kitchen.

CAITLIN THOMAS

I'm always shouting. That's how I keep my voice. But it's also probably why I can't keep a man.

SHIRLEY BASSEY

I've always found that the men who want to make love to you are never the ones you want. It's always some frightful little worm who cowers and grovels and lays himself out. Whenever I met a man like that I wanted to kick him.

CAITLIN THOMAS

THE MINES

Despite their ruined lungs, tobacco and snuff were as much a part of a miner's kit as his Davey lamp and a handful of sugar lumps for the pit ponies: a remedial pinch of snuff was the only thing that cleared the ponies' nostrils of coal dust.

ANNA SWAN

A miners' choir is as typical of Wales as a cricket match on an English meadow is of England.

H.V. MORTON

Considering I'm the son of a Welsh miner, one would expect me to be at my happiest playing peasants and people of the earth, but in actual fact I'm much happier playing princes and kings. Maybe it's sublimation.

RICHARD BURTON

The life of one Welsh miner is of greater commercial and moral value than the whole royal crowd put together.

KEIR HARDIE

The public weeps for the miners when there's an explosion, curses them when there's a strike, and forgets them the rest of the time.

JAMES GRIFFITHS

When the last truckload of coal reaches Cardiff, when the last black diamond is dug from the earth of Glamorgan, there will be men digging gems of pure brilliance from the inexhaustible mines of the language and literature of Wales.

MEREDITH JONES

Miners' Refuse To Work After Death.

Headline in **THE CAMBRIAN NEWS**

In south Wales there are more pubs than chapels and more coal mines than schools.

HOWARD MARKS

I was once challenged to a drinking contest by an entire rugby team, all of them Welsh miners. I got through 19 boilermakers – that's whiskey chased by a pint of beer – but the next day I was in no state to remember who won.

RICHARD BURTON

MONEY

The trustees of the Charlotte Church Fund allow her £445 a week on her cash card and £2,075 a month on her credit card. It's hardly rock star excess. The combined sum would scarcely make a dent in Elton John's weekly flower bill.

RICHARD BARBER

Money tormented him all his life and, with monstrous irony, like some bird of prey that had been gnawing at his liver, flew away as soon as he became a corpse.

CONSTANCE FITZGIBBON *on Dylan Thomas*

My father had the shortest will ever. It said: 'Being of sound mind, I spent all my money.'

TOMMY COOPER

They said I was worth $500 million. If that was true I wouldn't have visited Vietnam; I'd have sent for it.

BOB HOPE

The UK is in an economic crisis at the moment. Every cloud has a silver lining but we may have to eat it to stay afloat.

HARRY SECOMBE

Today I am worth $4 million more than I was yesterday.

RICHARD BURTON'S *alleged statement the day after he first slept with Elizabeth Taylor*

The other day my doctor told me I had low blood pressure but he promptly gave me something to raise it – the bill.

TOMMY COOPER

Is money the be-all and end-all that dictates the extent to which you can enjoy your life and experience for the first time a sense of dignity, bringing to an end an overwhelming feeling of self-loathing? I think so, yes.

KEITH BARRET

Never make the unpardonable error of thinking that it is romantic to be poor.

CAITLIN THOMAS

I was earning more as a hod-carrier than I was playing for Bury.

NEVILLE SOUTHALL

I've always tried to pay my bills with a smile, but they usually want money instead.

ALUN EDWARDS

For Dylan and myself it was always either the palace or the stable.

CAITLIN THOMAS

I keep meaning to write small plays but to hell with it. If I'm going to be broke all my life then I'm certainly not going to skimp on stage.

GREG CULLEN

The only thing Lloyd George wasn't prepared to do for the poor was to become one of them.

JENNIE LEE

Damn it all, you can't have the crown of thorns *and* the 30 pieces of silver.

ANEURIN BEVAN *on his position in the Labour Party in 1956*

If you have to ask the price, you can't afford it.

JOHN PIERPOINT MORGAN

I have always been honest and sincere in my literary work without thinking of popularity. That, I suppose, is why I have remained poor.

W.H. DAVIES

If she asks for a million dollars for a film, I demand a million plus ten. I've always believed a husband should have a larger pay packet than his wife.

RICHARD BURTON *on Liz Taylor*

I have seen people in the depth of despair because their money had run out so they couldn't buy food. They would go to the butcher's for bones for a dog they didn't have just to make some kind of stew.

BEATRICE WOOD

Prison places cost the US taxpayer more than university places.

HOWARD MARKS

I've been in London. Since I returned I've been very busy failing to make money.

DYLAN THOMAS

My folks were Welsh. We were too poor to be British.

BOB HOPE

What will I do with the money? Well I'd like to buy a car that goes around roundabouts without breaking down, and doesn't have moss in it.

RACHEL RICE *after winning* Big Brother 9

I am extremely poor at the moment. There is no chance of getting any money out of poetry. There are no literary dibbers, only a handful of grey-faced young men with private incomes and no inclination to give one anything but melancholia and dysentery.

DYLAN THOMAS

MORALITY

The infliction of cruelty with a good conscience is a delight to moralists. That is why they invented hell.

BERTRAND RUSSELL

Righteous people terrify me. Virtue is its own punishment.

ANEURIN BEVAN

Few people can tell a lie to your face with such perfect composure as a Welshman.

ARTHUR JOHNSON

The loss of sin is a loss to literature. Without sin we shall never have anything but lyrical poetry.

SAUNDERS LEWIS

It profits a man nothing to give his soul for the whole world – but for Wales!

ROBERT BOLT

It is easy enough to follow Christ. The difficulty is following his followers.

BEN BOWEN

Nowadays we suffer from an over-abundance of lawyers with an under-abundance of principles.

RAY MILLAND

If one sticks too rigidly to one's principles, one would hardly see anybody.

AGATHA CHRISTIE

I don't believe there is such a thing as a 'fallen woman'. I hate the smug fools who pass prostitutes by on the other side and I detest the blaggards who employ them and drop them. Real chastity is mental, not physical.

SAUNDERS LEWIS

A man with no vices usually has no virtues either.

ABRAHAM LINCOLN

Someone has defined a technicality as a point of principle which we have forgotten.

SIR ELWYN JONES

It has never yet occurred to me to deny myself a temptation because it might do me harm. That stipulation is, if anything, an added incentive to me.

CAITLIN THOMAS

I agree with Buddha that the essence of life is evil. Apart from not being born at all, it is best to die young.

DYLAN THOMAS

MOTIVATION

The reason I drink is because I will soon be dead and then won't be able to drink any more.

DYLAN THOMAS

I love her to bits but it also helped that her parents own a pub.

GAVIN HENSON *on his relationship with Charlotte Church*

Richard Burton never fought back, never excused himself, never said the critics were wrong, because in his heart he knew they were not. Marriage to Taylor tore him in two. He knew that fame and fortune would accrue. Half of him wanted that but the other half bitterly resented what he had done. So he drank.

RODERICK MANN

I was getting into my car and this bloke says to me, 'Could you give me a lift?' I said, 'You look great. The world's your oyster. Go for it.'

TOMMY COOPER

A shared fondness for P.G. Wodehouse, which we would read aloud to each other, is not a bad reason for staying with someone.

SIÂN PHILLIPS *on her marriage to Peter O'Toole*

I became an actor simply because I wanted to be famous. All the rest is hogwash.

ANTHONY HOPKINS

If players have to be doped to get them onto the field of play they ought to be painlessly put away. And if a hypodermic has to be used, I know what I'd do. I'd give them one prod in the right place and I wager they'd move faster than with any pep drugs.

TREVOR FORD

A Welshman doesn't need a reason to drink. All he needs is a drink.

GLYN ROBERTS

I once asked a woman why she wore a chemise in the bath when nobody could see her. 'Ah but God sees everything,' she replied.

BERTRAND RUSSELL

Love, anger, and the need for money.

DIC EDWARDS *on being asked what kept him going as a writer*

Ian Rush inspired a million youngsters to drink milk.

DYLAN EBENEZER

I told the team today that we had no option but to win. The only alternative was to dig a hole in the field and bury ourselves there.

GARETH EDWARDS *after a famous victory over England*

For my Oscar-winning role in *The Lost Weekend* I prepared myself by studying drunks and derelicts. I didn't have to go far. Half of my friends were boozers.

RAY MILLAND

I usually choose a film because of the script and the location. If it's a nice place to be I then look at all the noughts in the offer being made. Then I say yes, because it's better than working for a living.

ANTHONY HOPKINS

The first thing that attracted Elizabeth Taylor to me was my hangover.

RICHARD BURTON

A phone company rings me up and asks me if I'm interested in having a TV on my phone. I go, 'No, I've already got a TV'. I'm not interested in having a TV on my phone for the same reason I don't want a piss in my tumble drier.

MARK WATSON

Why do I drink? To burn up the flatness, the stale, empty dull deadness that one feels going onstage.

RICHARD BURTON

My next album is going to be Ukrainian folk so I won't have to do any promotion.

CHARLOTTE CHURCH

What happens ten yards from goal is frequently pre-decided by a kiss and a kindly word of encouragement in a suburban semi-detached villa three miles from the ground.

TREVOR FORD

MOVIES

I've never seen any of my movies except the first two.

RICHARD BURTON

After visiting Universal Studios I know I will struggle to take some movies seriously. We toured the back lot, including the lake where numerous naval actions had been fought, a huge painted sky at one end blocking out the structures. Our courier had a normal physique but picked up a boulder and tossed it aside. The bridge collapsed as our tram crossed over it but we kept on going undisturbed. Floods raged and fires roared, starting and stopping at the flick of a switch, and rain poured through the trees until someone turned off the tap.

HUGH LOUDON

When I was young I wanted to be in movies because I'd heard about the large portions served up by film location caterers.

DAWN FRENCH

After I made *The Silence of the Lambs* I could hardly stop at traffic lights without someone rolling down the window of their car, licking their lips and going, 'Had your dinner yet, Hannibal?'

ANTHONY HOPKINS

They only got two things right – the camels and the sand.

LOWELL THOMAS *on* Lawrence of Arabia

There's not much you can do with a bad movie. With a play you can tickle it, coax it into life. But when a movie is dead it stays dead.

RICHARD BURTON

The script was easy to learn because it consisted of just one word.

HARRY SECOMBE *on the film* Rhubarb, *that being the word*

Censorship was so bad when I was making *The Thin Man*, I had to use my neck like a turtle to squeeze in a love peck during a romantic scene.

MYRNA LOY

You have to make a lot of rubbish to pay the rent. My wife waited five years for a good script once. It got her the British Academy Award but she still waited three more years for another good one after that.

VINCENT PRICE

You're not a star in my profession until you're known as a monster.

BETTE DAVIS

Cinema was the most important medium of communication in the 1930s and 1940s. It presented Christmas six days a week every week, twice nightly.

HUGH LOUDON

You have to stay on your toes in the film business – like a midget at a urinal.

LESLIE NIELSON

Move those 10,000 horses a trifle to the right.

D.W. GRIFFITH, *allegedly, while directing an epic*

They say movies should be more like life. I think life should be more like the movies.

IOAN GRUFFUDD

Thank you. Your money's behind the washbasin.

TERRY JONES *to the jury who awarded him a prize at Cannes for* The Meaning of Life *in 1983*

In 1948 I refused to do a picture, the first and only time I was to take suspension in 21 years at Paramount. It was a turkey called *Bride of Vengeance*. I can still smell it. The critics lacerated it unmercifully and after five days of release it was yanked. The producer eventually migrated to England and is still there. I passed him on the street one day. I stuck out my hand to say hello and he cut me dead.

RAY MILLAND

I don't read reviews of my movies. If they're good they're not good enough and if they're bad it upsets me. So I don't bother with them.

RICHARD BURTON

The cinemas were magic places in my youth. For one shilling and three pence, and on Saturday afternoons two pence, Ronald Colman's smile beguiled you, Herbert Marshall limped into your heart, and Greta Garbo lured her lovers to destruction.

NESSIE WILLIAMS

Every movie is a wonderful success until it comes out.

STANLEY BAKER

MUSIC

Vinnie Jones' favourite group? Take That.

MICHAEL CULLEN

Girls Aloud is five dogs with no balls.

CHARLOTTE CHURCH

Sony completely owns us. They said if Manic Street Preachers want to smash the studio up it would make great press. Maybe, but we'd end up paying for it.

RICHEY EDWARDS

I knew from a very young age that my voice was a gift I should never abuse. When I'm on tour and doing a lot of back-to-back concerts I don't speak at all between performances. I just use sign language.

KATHERINE JENKINS

Our Sunday school music teacher was a cordial nymphomaniac who could make 'From Greenland's Icy Mountains' sound like a tropical rumba.

GWYN THOMAS

Tom Jones gets underpants and hotel keys thrown at him, I get Snoopy dolls.

BARRY MANILOW

'Karaoke' Kinnock will sing any song you want him to.

IAN LANG

We laughed when John Lennon got shot.

MANIC STREET PREACHERS

I believe it is the suppressed condition of the Welsh that is the reason why their music is so sentimental.

ROBERT AMBROSE JONES

If we Welsh are supposed to be a musical race, why aren't the acoustics better in the concrete urinals in the National Stadium?

GREN JONES

I inherited a painting and a violin which turned out to be a Rembrandt and a Stradivarius. Unfortunately, Rembrandt made lousy violins and Stradivarius was a terrible painter.

TOMMY COOPER

It was Welsh enough, wasn't it? There were only six of us singing 'Sospan Fach' but we made it sound like the national male voice choir.

GRAHAM JENKINS *to reporters at the funeral of his brother Richard Burton*

A vulgar caricature of showbiz success.

GEORGE MELLY *on Tom Jones*

A simple ballad can do more to tranquilize people than an aspirin or a bludgeon.

GWYN THOMAS

What's the difference between the Manic Street Preachers and Wales? Wales are still playing Giggs.

HUW JEFFARES

Singing in Wales is a spiritual interlude, something like prayer.

H.V. MORTON

Has Tom Jones had a hip replacement then?

SADIE RICHARDS

Where Englishmen hum or whistle, Welshmen open their chests, square their shoulders and sing as you can with no sounding board but the air.

RONALD BRYDEN

The reason Welshmen sing so much is because they don't have locks on their toilet doors.

LES DAWSON

I sing international pop with operatic overtones.

SHIRLEY BASSEY

I could never figure out whether John Cale wanted to be Elvis Presley, the Frankenstein monster or a young Chopin.

NAT FINKELSTEIN

At the Grammy Awards, Keith Richards became the first performer ever to accept a posthumous award in person.

JAY LENO

Opera is where a guy gets stabbed in the back and, instead of dying, he sings.

ROBERT BENCHLEY

My friends tell me that my rendering of a Scarlatti sonata sounds best from the garden.

WYNFORD VAUGHAN-THOMAS

For a time the Stones were in danger of becoming respectable.

KEITH RICHARDS

My second hit was a flop.

SHAKIN' STEVENS

Mam ruined more voices than any other teacher in the business.

IVOR NOVELLO *on his pedagogical mother*

What a horrible instrument the guitar is. It's worse than a mouth accordion, a Jew's harp or a paper and comb. It's worse than beating on nothing with a nought.

RICHARD BURTON

Adolf Hitler was one of the first rock stars. Look at the way he moved. He was easily as good as Mick Jagger. He staged a country.

DAVID BOWIE

Freddy Mercury stayed at number one for nine weeks with 'Bohemian Rhapsody'. In marriage terms this can't be far off a ruby wedding.

KEITH BARRET

They say 'sorry' is the hardest word to say but they're wrong. It's that Welsh railway station with the funny name.

HARRY SECOMBE

We've nicknamed Roy Keane 'Damien' after the character in *The Omen*.

RYAN GIGGS

Dear 338171, may I call you 338?

NOEL COWARD *in a military missive to T.E. Lawrence in 1930*

I was genuinely proud to be a Mrs Harrison although Rex had an unfortunate habit of treating me merely as the present holder of the title.

ELIZABETH HARRISON *on her husband, who married five times*

When a man writes his name on a professional form he signs away his liberty.

TREVOR FORD

I'm usually referred to these days as 'The ex-footballer-turned-actor'. I think what they would really like to say is 'The ex-crap-footballer-turned-actor'.

VINNIE JONES

The managing director of Hutchinson once complained to me, 'Your poetry books don't sell as well as those by Mary Wilson' [the Prime Minister's wife]. I was able to respond, 'Her name begins with W. Dwarfs read Mary Wilson. Giants read Dannie Abse.'

DANNIE ABSE

Engelbert Humperdinck's manager gave him that name as a gimmick. It's the same guy who managed Tom Jones. He was named after the movie. But at least Jones is a normal name, and the guy has a voice worth listening to.

RAY MILLAND

People keep telling me to change my name because nobody can spell it or pronounce it properly. That's what I like about it.

IOAN GRUFFUDD

An Englishman in Wales heard a cry for help from someone who had fallen into a ravine. 'Who is it?' he asked. 'Dafydd ap Gwilym ap Rhys ap Gruffydd ap Ifan ap Jenkins,' came the response. 'Well,' rejoined the Englishman, 'If there's half a dozen of you down there, you can jolly well pull one another out.'

CHRISTIE DAVIES

I killed stone dead the idea that a British heavyweight was another name for a horizontalist.

TOMMY FARR

I'm a member of a magic circle called the Secret Six. It's so secret I don't know the other five members.

TOMMY COOPER

I once applied for provisional driving licences in the names of Waylon Jennings and Elvis Presley. The Swansea computer didn't bat an eyelid. It didn't remember the 1950s.

HOWARD MARKS

Anthony Hopkins hates to be called 'Sir'. He told me to call him 'Lady' instead. I went, 'What are you, a duchess?'

JAMES WOODS

You need half a pint of phlegm in your throat to pronounce Welsh place-names.

HANNAH JONES

I didn't change my name from Zimmerman to Dylan because of Dylan Thomas. If I thought he was that great I would have sung his poems. I could just as easily have changed my name to Thomas.

BOB DYLAN

When U2 started, people referred to Bono as Bon Smelly Arse. I'm glad that didn't stick or things might have been different.

THE EDGE

I like England but not Britain.

EDWARD THOMAS

Interviewers often describe me to my face as 'rotund' or 'ample', never fat or big. That's far more offensive.

DAWN FRENCH

I'm still referred to as 'The King' by a garage owner in the parish of Llanigon. He's an Ayatollah and his chief mechanic is a Duke.

RICHARD BOOTH

If you ever wondered where all the Davieses came from, there's a big factory outside Bridgend with a sign outside saying, 'Davies Manufacturing Company'.

CHRISTIE DAVIES

That Robespierre of the raspberries.

WYNFORD VAUGHAN-THOMAS *on Gwynfor Evans, former MP for Carmarthen who was also a market gardener*

The definition of a Welsh peer is Senataff. A dead Welsh peer is an Epitaff.

CHRISTIE DAVIES

Humphrey Bogart's middle name was DeForest. Imagine it. *Casablanca* starring Ingrid Bergman and Humphrey DeForest Bogart. I told him with a name like that he could make a career in soap opera.

RICHARD BURTON

I've been accused of taking my surname from the Welsh poet Dylan Thomas. That's just a rumour put about by people who like to simplify things. It actually comes from an ancestor of mine who spelled his name 'Dillon'. I've done much more for Dylan Thomas than he's done for me. Look how many kids are probably reading his poetry today because they heard I took my name from him.

BOB DYLAN

If I had a penny for every time I've been called Ronald I would be the richest writer in Wales.

ROALD DAHL

Names aren't always what they seem. The common Welsh name 'BZJXXLLWCP', for instance, is pronounced 'Jackson'.

MARK TWAIN

Last night I dreamed I was eating a 10-pound marshmallow. When I woke up this morning the pillow was gone.

TOMMY COOPER

Over 100 years ago, a man in Worcester ate 152 pounds of plums at one sitting.

DYLAN THOMAS

No, I came home stone-cold sober and when I got into it, the bed was already on fire.

RICHARD BOOTH *after being accused of setting his bed on fire one night when he was drunk*

The main problem with the Welsh is that they're all behind you to your face but behind your back they're at your throat.

KEITH BARRET

The Post Office sought permission to erect telephone poles on the Llanfoist housing site. They have been told that whilst the Council do not object to the installation of telephones, they consider the poles should be laid underground.

ABERGAVENNY CHRONICLE

I think inventions are marvellous, don't you? Wherever they put a petrol pump they find petrol.

TOMMY COOPER

To talk a great deal of nonsense is good if you can listen to it also.

SAUNDERS LEWIS

I once passed a hole in the road from which I could hear council workmen singing, 'Happy birthday to you, Happy birthday to you'. I enquired whose birthday it was and was told, 'It's the hole's. He's one today.'

MAX BOYCE

'Waiter, waiter, this coffee tastes like tea.'
'Sorry sir, I must have brought you cocoa by mistake.'

TOMMY COOPER

The late F.W. Myers once asked a man at a dinner table what he thought would happen to him when he died. The man tried to ignore the question but on being pressed replied, 'Oh well I suppose I shall inherit eternal bliss – but I wish you wouldn't talk about such unpleasant subjects.'

BERTRAND RUSSELL

I celebrated my 21st birthday when I was 22.

MEIC STEVENS

I have to go now, but stay as long as you like.

AUGUSTUS JOHN to *Adrian Daintrey after inviting him to his house*

A little nonsense now and then is cherished by the wisest men.

ROALD DAHL

Pwyll said to Twm: 'That man has been sitting there doing nothing for hours.' 'How do you know?' asked Twm. 'I've been sitting here watching him.'

WYNFORD JONES

Give me the luxuries of life and I'll willingly do without the necessities.

FRANK LLOYD WRIGHT

It took a lot of willpower but I've finally given up trying to stop smoking.

TOMMY COOPER

Why do they advertise TVs on TV? If I didn't have one how could I see the advert?

LEE EVANS

My humour is quite Welsh, although I don't quite know what I mean by that.

RHOD GILBERT

There's more sense in nonsense than there's nonsense in sense.

CLEDWYN WILLIAMS

I speak mathematics like a native.

HARRY SECOMBE

I can go into people's brains and turn all the taps on so the water floods out of their ears, their nose and their mouth. In the end they go insane.

LAUREN HARRIES

If you think there's a part of Europe called East Angular, and if you're capable of the sentence 'Rio de Janeiro, ain't he a person?' are you really going to be a paragon of political correctness?

ROS WYNNE-JONES *on Jade Goody*

What genius came up with the scoring system in darts: 'First one to nothing wins!'

LEE EVANS

I went to the dentist. He said my teeth were all right but my gums had to come out.

TOMMY COOPER

OBSESSIONS

During our engagement several members of our families gloomily foretold that Mary's lack of interest in horses would be the downfall of our marriage but from the first it was a joke between us and through the years we have found it has balanced my own single-minded concentration into a shared sense of proportion.

DICK FRANCIS

I'm told that the first step to curing any addiction is to admit it. So here goes. My name is Carol Vorderman and I'm addicted to Sudoku.

CAROL VORDERMAN

To anyone with politics in his blood, this place is like a pub to a drunkard.

DAVID LLOYD GEORGE *on the House of Commons*

Retirement terrifies me because I don't have any hobbies.

TOM JONES

Actors are poor, abject, disagreeable, perverse, ill-minded, slightly malicious creatures. They must have the centre of the stage or at least the second centre. They'd like to stop but they can't. And of that august company of idiots, I'm afraid I'm a member.

RICHARD BURTON

His obsession with his own demise was macabre; he would telephone me and, pretending to be a policeman, announce his death or near death in some accident or other.

ELIZABETH HARRISON *on a strange peccadillo of her ex-husband Richard Harris*

My father was a football fanatic. I remember my mother once shaking her head and muttering, 'If footballs were edible he'd eat one with every meal and not bother with a knife and fork.'

TREVOR FORD

The only thing in life is language. Not love, not anything else.

RICHARD BURTON

Writing poetry is the best way I know of untying the knot of obsession. It's cheaper than therapy and better for you than getting drunk.

GWYNETH LEWIS

PARENTHOOD

The whole industry behind motherhood treats mothers as imbeciles. They keep telling us we need stuff. Just get yourself a buggie and some nappies. Everything else is crap.

CERYS MATHEWS

I never heard my father recite a line from a poem.

DANNIE ABSE

I am a Welsh aristocrat. In a good light I can trace my ancestry all the way back to my father.

GWYN THOMAS

A two-year-old doesn't leave you alone just because you're nursing a hangover.

RYAN GIGGS *on the delights of being a father*

My therapist and I have really bonded. He hates my father as well now.

TERENCE DAVIES

In the last years when he was falling apart under the weight of his own legend, his father must have looked at him with the grey-eyed amazement of the stricken Faustus, trying to find resemblances to himself in the demonic force he had conjured up from the sea of his own incurable yearnings.

GWYN THOMAS

Phil Burton didn't adopt me. I adopted Phil Burton.

RICHARD BURTON *on the man who gave him his name*

He had a foolproof system for developing his tales. He would tell them to his children and if they asked to hear one again he knew he had a winner.

PATRICIA NEAL *on her husband Roald Dahl*

'Sunshine for your grandchildren' is a bad electoral programme.

DAVID LLOYD GEORGE

'Are you sure this is real Welsh lamb?' said the angry customer to her butcher. 'Well, Mrs Jenkins, it was really born in New Zealand but I can assure you it had Welsh parents.'

CHRISTIE DAVIES

We all have our breaking points, don't we? Put a gun to the head of any one of my children and I'll tell you all I know. But threaten me with a prison term and I'll tell you to f★★★ off.

HOWARD MARKS

Two little boys in Hollywood were having a conversation. One of them said, 'I bet my Dad can beat your Dad'. The other replied, 'Your Dad *is* my Dad'.

EMLYN WILLIAMS

The father is the head of the family and the mother the heart.

HUW *from* How Green Was My Valley

Father doesn't hear what mother says, and mother hears what father does not say.

CAROL DAVIES

We can't really get to know our father as other people do until we are almost grown up ourselves, but by then he has become that immutable bundle of fixed opinions and uncurious appetites – the middle-aged man.

GRIFF RHYS JONES

PEOPLE AND PLACES

What do you call a sheep tied to a lamp-post in Cardiff? A leisure centre.

ROB BRYDON

Pontypridd is the Damascus of Glamorgan.

GWYN THOMAS

Dreadful thought, London. Rain and coughs and colds and all those ugly pinched discontented cheerless faces, and the frightful press.

RICHARD BURTON

I rang up the local swimming baths. I said, 'Is that the local swimming baths?' He said, 'It depends where you're calling from.'

TOMMY COOPER

One feels on seeing Cardiff for the first time as one feels when meeting some congenial and charming person of whom one has heard nothing but slander.

H.V. MORTON

London is an impersonal city. I've been here ten years now but I still haven't met anyone.

RHOD GILBERT

The Cardiff accent's a sort of Welsh cockney, spoken out of the corner of the mouth.

MICHAEL ASPEL

I think of Wales as my wife and London as my mistress.

DANNIE ABSE

Until you've lived in Wales you don't know what cheerfulness is.

LAURA ASHLEY

Our house in Laugharne is a wrecked, wracked shack, adrift with water and manned by rats, sunk in the leaking navel of Wales and less comfortable than a crucifix.

CAITLIN THOMAS

I moved from New York to L.A. to get away from drugs but it was ten times worse there.

JOHN CALE

To those who believe the New Zealander lacks a sense of humour, I suggest they read the sign in Auckland Airport's departure lounge which bears the following request: 'Will the last person leaving the country please put the lights out?'

MAX BOYCE

I was a bit shocked when I discovered the Italians didn't put sugar and milk in their tea, but rather slices of lemon.

JOHN CHARLES *after joining Juventus*

The morning after we arrived in Beirut I leaned out of my hotel window and in the street below two men from the surrounding hills shot a young girl, a family member who'd brought disgrace on them by descending to a life of sin in the big city. 'What'll happen to them?' I asked. 'Nothing,' I was told, 'It's their right.'

SIÂN PHILLIPS

Richard has never been allowed into Ireland and Dickie never left it.

ELIZABETH HARRISON *on the schizophrenic nature of her first husband, Richard Harris*

The East German manages to combine a Teutonic capacity for bureaucracy with a Russian capacity for infinite delay.

GORONWY REES

L.A. is disgusting and wonderful.

ALAN RICKMAN

The Rhondda Valley – where men are men and sheep are nervous.

GRAFFITI

In Merthyr you were judged by how fast you put the kettle on the range.

ANNA SWAN

What is Calais but Dover in reverse?

ANN RUTHERFORD

Anglesey is one enormous farm.

H.V. MORTON

Those English – you make one perfectly normal request at a normal volume and they pucker their rectums.

DAWN FRENCH

One in five people in the world are Chinese. There are five people in my family so it must be one of them. It's either my mum or my dad or my older brother Colin or my younger brother Ho-Cha-Chu. But I think it's Colin.

TOMMY COOPER

Actors are freaks in America and Hollywood is all freaksville.

VINCENT PRICE

It is ridiculous to set a detective story in New York City. New York City is *itself* a detective story.

AGATHA CHRISTIE

There won't be any revolution in America. The people are too clean. They spend all their time changing their shirts and washing themselves. You can't feel fierce and revolutionary in a bathroom.

ERIC LINKLATER

Two things a Frenchman will always give you – good manners and directions to the nearest public toilet. That's about it.

RAY MILLAND

Beverly Hills has got a slum area. It's called the rest of the world.

BOB HOPE

Pontrhydyfen is the birthplace of Richard Burton and the graveyard of coal. According to local wits the village cemetery, beside the stone church on the hilltop, is the dead centre.

JOHN COTTRELL

Monmouthshire is a county that has spent much of its time cuddling Wales while playing footsie with England.

TREVOR FISHLOCK

My father thought Hollywood was a small place somewhere on the other side of the Welsh mountains.

RICHARD BURTON

Yuppies are turning Wales into a giant theme park. They're thinking of putting turnstiles up between the Brecon Beacons and converting Bridgend into a crèche.

BILL SHIPTON

A. My wife's gone to the Welsh border.

B. Wye?'

A. Search me.

INTERNET JOKE

When Dylan succumbed to the scavenging spawn of America I knew it was the end of me. And, not too long after, the fatal end of him.

CAITLIN THOMAS

The Welsh in Cardiff take pains to hide their origin.

CARODOC EVANS

Americans believe all their problems can be solved by acid tablets and nappies.

EDWARD THOMAS

The Italians, from long years of poverty, always put 'bella' before whatever insufficiency they have to eat to make it that more appetising.

CAITLIN THOMAS

Swansea now finds itself wondering, much as it did at the beginning of the 19th century, what is the reason for its existence: industry and commerce, trade and transport, or leisure and tourism?

NIGEL JENKINS

This arsehole of the universe.

DYLAN THOMAS *on his native Laugharne*

Augustus John once injured his neck by diving onto an unexpected rock in Tenby. He emerged from convalescence a genius in the Renaissance mould. Tenby Bay from now on will be full of bathers plunging fearlessly onto rocks, hoping to concuss themselves into supernormal talent.

GWYN THOMAS

New York is a place where a starving man could have 34 television sets in his basement.

RICHARD BOOTH

Holyhead is a dwindling little place, no longer even somewhere on the way to somewhere else.

BYRON ROGERS

It was a typical old English country house: 56 rooms and a bath. It was a strange kind of bath – it went all round the place. It was called a moat.

BOB HOPE

I am only a bit of a Welshman in an office in London.

DAVID LLOYD GEORGE

Hamburg: birthplace of The Beatles, but surprisingly not the hamburger.

KEITH BARRET

I've just come back from three dark days in London, city of the restless dead. It really is an insane city and it filled me with terror. Every pavement drills through your soles to your scalp and out pops a lamp-post covered with hair.

DYLAN THOMAS

POETRY

Dylan Thomas once told me that poets only know two kinds of birds by sight. One is a robin and the other a seagull. The rest they have to look up.

LAWRENCE DURRELL

When a poet begins to write a poem there is no reader. As he concludes it, he becomes the first one. And perhaps the last.

DANNIE ABSE

Adjectives are the betrayers of poetry, the poet's chief enemies.

SAUNDERS LEWIS

Given the choice between latex and holly, the poet, at least for a short sit-down, would take holly.

GWYN THOMAS

The reason most people don't care for poetry is because most poets don't care much for people.

TONY CURTIS *(the poet, not the actor)*

More people write poetry than read it.

R.S. THOMAS

If well-meaning friends wanted an abstruse interpretation of some of Dylan's more obscure lines which he had long ago forgot the meaning of himself, it wasn't long before he was on the floor wrapped up in the carpet, scratching himself like a flea-bitten hyena in paroxysms of acute boredom.

CAITLIN THOMAS

If I knew certainly that what I wrote was poetry and not tosh, I don't think I should be at all very anxious to give it to the world. I should be satisfied with the mere achievement.

SAUNDERS LEWIS

What's the point of an ambition to write the next poem, then the one after? Would it not be more valuable to conjure toy sailing boats into glass bottles?

DANNIE ABSE

When I was six I decided I was going to be a poet.

TERRY JONES

Poetry is trouble dunked in tears.

GWYN THOMAS

At the age of 20 you are not yet born as a poet.

R.S. THOMAS

Yeats taught the lyric poet to grow old.

VERNON WATKINS

In England if you say you're a poet it's as if you have a personal hygiene problem.

GWYNETH LEWIS

Writing a poem you're not even sure what you're looking for, just that something is out there wild and running and for some reason you're not quite sure of you have to run after it.

DERYN REES-JONES

It's not poetry just because the lines don't reach the end of the page.

VERNON WATKINS

If Seamus Heaney belonged to an unfashionable race, were he a Welshman for instance, his poetry would have been lucky to have made it into the parish magazine.

A.N. WILSON

Dylan Thomas was a slob, a liar, a moocher, a thief, a two-fisted booze fighter, a puffy Priapus who regularly assaulted the wives of his best friends, an icy little hedonist who indifferently lived it up while his children went hungry. Though he looked like a choirboy, he argued like a Bolshevik, dressed like a bum, drank like a culvert and smoked like an ad for cancer.

TIME *magazine*

The only nice poets I've met were bad poets and a bad poet is not a poet at all. Ergo, I've never met a nice poet.

RICHARD BURTON

POLITICS

I've been known to sit next to Tony Blair and natter away with him no differently from the way I'd chat to the lads at the local.

VINNIE JONES

A political commentator mused once, 'If you want to get the feelings of the Tories or the Labour Party about a particular issue you take soundings among half a dozen MPs. But if you want to find out something about Wales you have to ask all 35 of them.

TREVOR FISHLOCK

I can still remember the day when I encountered my first Conservative, a shock all the greater in that it coincided with the crisis of puberty.

GWYN WILLIAMS

David Lloyd George can't see a belt without hitting below it.

MARGOT ASQUITH

Fascism is not in itself a new order of society. It is the future refusing to be born.

ANEURIN BEVAN

Patriots always talk of dying for their country but never of killing for it.

BERTRAND RUSSELL

When one nation begins to imitate another it is the lowest and worst things that are usually imitated.

GRIFFITH JOHN WILLIAMS

The dissident is the key figure of our time.

EMYR HUMPHREYS

Welsh folk are so obsequious they're grateful to the English for tolerating one of us as their Prime Minister.

SAUNDERS LEWIS *on David Lloyd George*

The reason I played Churchill so well was because I knew his secret: he was the greatest actor of them all.

RICHARD BURTON

Ninety-five per cent of Welsh people are honest, law-abiding folk. It's the other five per cent we need to worry about. But then we elected them.

DAI WILLIAMS

Tories do believe in reform, but not yet.

CLEDWYN LLOYD

The younger generation have less instinctive loyalty to the Labour Party. They know, and want to know, little about the bitter struggles of the past. Eligible to vote at 18, they seek, not to understand the party that was born in sweat, blood and tears on a mountainside near Merthyr.

MAGGIE PRYCE JONES

Aneurin Bevan dealt with reality by shuffling dreams. He was the eternal gatecrasher who dared to question the existence of the gates.

DAI SMITH

Passionately-held political convictions are likely to unhinge one who sets himself up as a literary critic, especially if he lacks a sense of humour.

DANNIE ABSE

If Richard Burton had taken up politics I would have expected him to end up as Prime Minister.

DONALD HOUSTON

If you want to succeed in politics you must learn to keep your conscience under control.

DAVID LLOYD GEORGE

Loyalty is a fine quality but in excess it fills political graveyards.

NEIL KINNOCK *on devolution*

Politicians don't have to fool all the people all the time, just the majority of them at election time.

HARRY SECOMBE

There is no friendship at the top.

DAVID LLOYD GEORGE

I liked what I knew about [Neil] Kinnock. Would he turn out to be the long-awaited combination of King Arthur, Owain Glendower and Nye Bevan that would oust the Iron Lady Thatcher and become our new Prime Minister?

HOWARD MARKS

Every man has a House of Lords in his own head. Fears, prejudices, misconceptions – these are the peers and they are hereditary.

DAVID LLOYD GEORGE

The trouble with the Socialist Workers' Party is that it lives in a historical thermos flask.

NEIL KINNOCK

Don't vote – the government always gets in.

CLEDWYN ELLIS

I would die for my country but I could never let my country die for me.

NEIL KINNOCK *on the nuclear threat*

Winston Churchill spoiled himself by reading about Napoleon.

DAVID LLOYD GEORGE

If Boris Johnson becomes mayor it will be a case of the lunatic having no idea how to run the asylum.

ALAN RICKMAN

Mrs Teal: Are you standing in a by-election, Dafydd?
Dafydd: It's not just a bi-election. It's for gays and straights too.

LITTLE BRITAIN

POLITICAL INVECTIVE

It's amazing how wise great statesmen can be when it's ten years too late.

DAVID LLOYD GEORGE

The trouble with Michael Heseltine is that he has had to buy all his furniture.

ALAN CLARK

One should tolerate the Labour Government because running down Labour eventually brings you alongside the Conservatives, which is the last place you want to be.

DYLAN THOMAS

Neil Kinnock has the consistency of a chameleon and the wisdom of a weathercock.

MICHAEL HOWARD

Hugh Gaitskell was the right kind of leader for the Labour Party – a desiccated calculating machine.

ANEURIN BEVAN

I can think of only one European nation which is governed as badly as Wales and that is Brittany, where the French Government is deliberately trying to destroy the nation.

GWYNFOR EVANS

David Lloyd George was a blatant hypocrite but he's forgiven a lot in Wales because he proved that a Welshman brought up in the chapels could not only out-talk, out-drink and out-fornicate any Englishman but also run the Englishman's country better than he could himself.

JOHN RICHARDS

Welsh councillor: 'I'm not really in favour of local elections. They introduce an element of uncertainty into the council's business.'

CHRISTIE DAVIES

I wonder if Neil Kinnock exists at all or if he is some plastic puppet squeezed into shape by his PR experts and by trade union leaders, or whoever bullied him last.

NORMAN TEBBIT

The SDLP have policies like liquid grease.

NEIL KINNOCK

The soul of most conservatism is sentimentality and sentimentality preserves the good and the bad with equal relish.

GWYN THOMAS

If you vote for Kinnock you're voting against Christ.

BARBARA CARTLAND *in 1992*

Nigel Lawson could be bundled into a political dustbin without a squeak of protest from the voters, the City or even the Conservative Party. He is not a Chancellor. He is a manikin with a thick coating of bombast.

ROY JENKINS

If you were hanging from a ledge by your fingers, James Callaghan would stamp on them.

EDWARD PEARCE

The tiger that was once the king of the jungle is now just the fireside rug.

GORDON BROWN *on Michael Heseltine's decline*

There are two ways of getting into the Cabinet. One is to crawl up the stairway of preferment on your belly. The other way is to kick them in the teeth.

ANEURIN BEVAN

A politician is a person with whose politics you don't agree. If you agree with him, he's a statesman.

DAVID LLOYD GEORGE

Neil Kinnock has a proven ability to conceal his immaturity under pressure.

NORMAN TEBBIT

They died with their drawn salaries in their hands.

DAVID LLOYD GEORGE *on the 1905 Tory Government*

Tony Benn couldn't knock the skin off a rice pudding.

NEIL KINNOCK

In Kinnock Britain has at last produced a party leader worthy of assassination.

BRYN EDWARDS

Nigel Lawson is to economic forecasting what Eddie the Eagle is to ski-jumping.

NEIL KINNOCK

There'll be no need for wind farms once the Welsh Assembly gets going. There will be enough hot air to keep the principality lit up night and day.

THE TIMES

Douglas Haig was brilliant to the top of his army boots.

DAVID LLOYD GEORGE

If I could only piss the way David Lloyd George speaks.

GEORGES CLÉMENCEAU

Born into the ranks of the working class, King George V's most likely fate would have been that of street-corner loafer.

JAMES KEIR HARDIE

The last time Ireland was faced with a terrorist threat of magnitude was in the aftermath of the Twin Towers atrocity. It trembled at the prospect of Osama bin Laden crashing a plane into Sellafield and contaminating the Emerald Isle with radioactive fall-out. Nobody was too concerned about Wales, oddly enough.

DAVID KENNY

All Arthur Balfour will leave behind in history is the scent of a pocket handkerchief.

DAVID LLOYD GEORGE

I've just heard that Aneurin Bevan is ill. I hope it's nothing trivial.

WINSTON CHURCHILL

David Lloyd George didn't care which direction the car was travelling in as long as he stayed in the driver's seat.

LORD BEAVERBROOK

Does a one-legged duck swim in circles?

RHODRI MORGAN *after being asked by Jeremy Paxman if he would like to be the Labour leader of the new Welsh Assembly*

Welsh Labour councillors are all the same. They're short, they're fat, and they're fundamentally corrupt.

ROD RICHARDS *MP, former Junior Welsh Office minister*

PRAISE

When Elizabeth [Taylor] was present she had more presence than anyone else. Since we went our separate ways I've found no one's absence could be so absent.

RICHARD BURTON

Living in a goldfish bowl isn't living at all. Adulation is alienating me from the human race.

BARRY JOHN

Kevin Ratcliffe is the Carl Lewis of Goodison – unbeatable over short distances.

ANDY GRAY

He stands by himself, a lonely figure, king of the land of wicked fairies disguised as chapel-goers.

WYN GRIFFITH *on Caradoc Evans*

If there were 12 elephants on a stage and Richard Burton was there too, you'd look at Burton.

RICHARD HARRIS

There should be a statue of John Charles outside every football ground to remind footballers what they can aspire to.

MICHAEL PARKINSON

Dylan Thomas could read the telephone book and make it sound like scripture.

JAMES DICKEY

He did everything without looking as if he even broke sweat.

WILL CARLING *on Barry John*

Cayo Evans is better at the blarney than I am.

BRENDAN BEHAN

Tommy Cooper could reduce audiences to hysterics by just coughing behind the curtain before he even went on stage.

TREVOR MCDONALD

Richard Burton could make silence garrulous.

KENNETH TYNAN

He could play snooker with a broom handle.

RAY REARDON *on Alex Higgins in his prime*

He was the show. The show was him. He had me rolling on the floor laughing most days.

CAROL VORDERMAN *on* Countdown *host Richard Whiteley, who died in 2005*

Her authority was so complete she never had to lose her temper like I did. If she told you not to do something you didn't do it and you didn't argue. She always gave orders with a smile, but the more she smiled the more quickly you acted.

BERNARD ASHLEY *on his famous wife Laura*

Marlene Dietrich is the most beautiful woman I've ever met. She's like a skeleton risen from the grave, her face bones barely covered with make-up. Arise, oh beautiful bones. And she cooks well, too.

RICHARD BURTON

Adulation is easier to relinquish than hate. We have no heroes now and it is too painful to give up our villains.

LEO ABSE

Dylan Thomas had the faculty of becoming a part of people's lives almost before he knew them.

VERNON WATKINS

PUBLICITY

With the newspaper strike on, I wouldn't even consider it.

BETTE DAVIS *after being informed there was a rumour going around that she'd died*

It's nice to get stabbed in the front for a change.

TERRY VENABLES *on the Australian media*

Sooner or later a public figure becomes a public bore or a public joke.

RICHARD BURTON

Anytime he went to the loo there was a photographer waiting for him there.

DESMOND LLEWELYN *on Sean Connery during the filming of* You Only Live Twice

My pet hate was the publicity department. You were often asked to attend openings and exhibitor meetings. I got out of most of those by having a relative die suddenly. I honestly believe I had more relatives kick the bucket than any individual west of the Rockies.

RAY MILLAND

It's dangerous to believe your own publicity. Sometimes I'm embarrassed to see my name above a film. I find it hard to take it in. I try to preserve my self-doubt to keep myself grounded.

ANTHONY HOPKINS

'Press' is all too often made up of two words: 'pry' and 'mess'. They're too busy looking for headlines – or bedlines.

BETTE DAVIS

The audience were with me all the way but I managed to shake them off at the train station.

HARRY SECOMBE

And then there were the two cannibals who ate a clown. One said to the other, 'Does this taste funny to you?'

TOMMY COOPER

I shall miss the marriages of all my various children and they'll be angry because there'll be nobody, apart from their mother, to make bad puns.

RICHARD BURTON *on the prospect of dying young from drink*

My wife and I got married in a toilet. It was a marriage of convenience.

TOMMY COOPER

What are your chances of winning if you can keep Henson out of Church?

SUE BARKER *to Mike Ruddock about a forthcoming rugby match in 2006*

Roy Jenkins tended to knock off at seven o'clock. He was more of a socialite than a socialist.

HAROLD MACMILLAN

A knight to forget.

CLIVE BARNES' *evaluation of Richard Burton in* Camelot *in Toronto in 1980*

Police arrested two children yesterday. One was drinking battery acid and the second was eating fireworks. They charged one and let the other one off.

TOMMY COOPER

You'd think if any team could put up a decent wall it would be China.

TERRY VENABLES *after that country made a defensive lapse against Brazil during the 2002 World Cup*

Welcome to the Academy Awards. Or, as it's known in our house, Passover.

BOB HOPE

Wales gave us Catherine Zeta-Jones and Dylan Thomas. A great pair. And Thomas wasn't bad either.

ANTHONY TORMEY

Always approach a problem with a try angle.

ROY NOBLE

I went to the butcher's the other day and bet him £50 be couldn't reach the meat on his top shelf. He refused to take the bet. He said the steaks were too high.

TOMMY COOPER

Prince Charles is wise beyond his ears.

ARMAND HAMMER

I wish we could chat longer but I'm having an old friend for dinner.

ANTHONY HOPKINS*'s last line as Hannibal Lecter in* The Silence of the Lambs

I heard a rumour that Dawn French was arrested for smuggling drugs at Cardiff Airport. Apparently the customs officer asked her to bend over and he says he saw 50 pounds of crack.

ALED LEWIS

If it's not one thing it's your mother.

IAN WATKINS

I got home the other night and the wife was crying her eyes out. I said, 'What's the matter?" She said, 'I'm homesick'. I said, 'This *is* your home'. She said, 'I know. I'm sick of it'.

TOMMY COOPER

RAIN

It's been raining in Wales since last June.

DYLAN THOMAS *in March 1951*

Welsh rain descends with the enthusiasm of someone breaking bad news. It comes down in a constant cataract. It runs round corners with the wind. It finds its way up your sleeves and down your neck. It sings a song on the roads as it runs to join other rivulets and form a little mountain torrent.

H.V. MORTON

One of the main reasons I became a poet was because it was always raining when I was a child and my mother wouldn't let me out in it. She gave me a pencil and paper instead.

DYLAN THOMAS

It never rains but it Ranchipurs.

RICHARD BURTON *summing up one of his most dire movies,* The Rains of Ranchipur

After a childhood spent strapping on lifebelts made of the more buoyant sheet-music in drenched eisteddfod marquees, I am gloomy about the sky when jollity is on the agenda.

GWYN THOMAS

A naked people under an acid rain.

GWYN WILLIAMS *on the Welsh*

I don't understand why it's still raining – the weekend is over.

TOMMY COOPER

If you can see the coast of Devon from Swansea it's going to rain. If you can't, it's raining already.

TRADITIONAL SAYING

Welsh humour is dry, which is more than can be said for the weather.

BILL SHIPTON

The best way to make it rain in Wales is to wash the car.

MYFANWY WILLIAMS

In the Bible God made it rain for 40 days and 40 nights. That's a pretty good summer for us in Wales. I was eight before I realised you could take a cagoule off.

RHOD GILBERT

RELIGION

Most people's idea of religion is a sentimental antidote to the hard realities of life.

SAUNDERS LEWIS

In terms of sheer praying power, Wales must have a handsome credit balance in heaven.

TREVOR FISHLOCK

When I was abusing Tequila Sunrises in my mad drinking days I had some semi-religious experiences. On one occasion I thought I was John the Baptist talking to the sea. And the sea talked back…

ANTHONY HOPKINS

I once knew a cannibal who was converted to Catholicism. On Fridays he only ate fishermen.

TOMMY COOPER

Church sermons were always too deep for me. I brought sports books into the pews and picked world teams.

GARETH EDWARDS

The truth of religion is in its ritual. The truth of dogma is in its poetry.

JOHN COWPER POWYS

The good news is that Jesus is coming back. The bad news is that he's really pissed off.

BOB HOPE

I once meant to write a book on the background of Christ. As good as Renan's *Life of Jesus* should have been if only he had the wit to leave out the central figure.

T.E. LAWRENCE

Religion in Wales has gone from dissent to absent.

GRAFFITI

I was brought up a Catholic but this remains the only religious experience I have ever had.

GREG CULLEN

I keep my copy of the Bible on a shelf next to Voltaire. Poison and antidote.

BERTRAND RUSSELL

If Moses had been a committee, the Israelites would still be in Egypt.

J.B. HUGHES

That's America for you. They won't let kids play in school but they put Bibles in motels.

BOB HOPE

What struck me most about the Crusades was how much they cribbed from Monty Python.

TERRY JONES

Ralph Ingersoll said no man with humour ever invented a religion. He should have added that he might have needed it, considering some of the ones we've seen.

GLYN ROBERTS

If you fail to be stirred by the Welsh landscape you will never get to heaven.

TREVOR FISHLOCK

In Wales, Methodists are divided into two groups: the galvanised Methodists and the wee sly ones.

DAFYDD JONES

Buildings and their maintenance seem of greater importance to the hierarchy today than empty seats. Priests who ought to be getting their lost sheep and bringing them home to their Father's house waste their time and energy on administration.

MAGGIE PRYCE JONES

A living paganism is much nearer to heaven than a dead religion.

D.J. WILLIAMS

The weak rely on Christ. The strong do not.

RICHARD BURTON

The trouble with being an atheist is that when something goes right there's no one to say thank you to.

ANNA SWAN

If there's nothing beyond death, nobody ever knows. Maybe there is, so we've got it both ways.

ANTHONY HOPKINS

A bishop usually has a redder nose and a larger belly than a curate.

W.H. DAVIES

My grandmother read the Bible daily. It was said that if all the Bibles in the village were burned, she would probably have been able to write out the whole of the Old Testament.

SIÂN PHILLIPS

If people knew how much ill-feeling unselfishness occasions, it would not be recommended so often from the pulpit.

C.S. LEWIS

The preacher's sermons were like water to a drowning man.

SELWYN LEWIS

Church-going declines not so much because of unbelief but because Dad has made a down-payment on the car.

ALAN JONES

A Welshman once built a town and put two chapels in it. Asked why he had built the second one, he replied, 'That's the one I don't go to'.

DAI RICHARDS

Whenever I get really down I start getting religious. The American Christian Right had thrown me off Christianity. If God was a Republican, forget it.

HOWARD MARKS

Baptists put the 'protest' into Protestantism.

ANNA SWAN

Being a Jew, I have to balance my love for the land of my fathers against my love for the land of my fathers' fathers.

STELLA LEVEY

I was frequently told off for asking the wrong kinds of questions at school. The one I remember most vividly was: 'When St Paul wrote all those letters to the Corinthians, did they ever write back?'

ANNA SWAN

I loved Pope John Paul II but I'm not too keen on his successor. Pope Benedict wants to ban Harry Potter because he says it's full of witchcraft. If he actually bothered to sit down and read it he would understand the morals of it.

CHARLOTTE CHURCH

I once thought of becoming a preacher but it was pointed out to me that I had no religious feelings. So I gave up the idea.

RICHARD BURTON

Auschwitz made me more of a Jew than Moses.

DANNIE ABSE

The innocent will always suffer since the first innocent was crucified.

MAGGIE PRYCE JONES

I once heard a Welsh sermon in which the word 'truth' was repeatedly uttered in English. Apparently there's no exact equivalent in Welsh.

GEOFFREY MADAN

Christ was a rash and splendid Peter Pan who was killed because a real child is a danger to all classes who are timid of the glory of joy.

SAUNDERS LEWIS

I am relieved that entry to heaven doesn't hinge on a Welsh victory in Dublin because I would be an even bet to end up in a warm climate.

GARETH EDWARDS

My concept of heaven is silence – and me dusting.

KYLIE MINOGUE

Cold beer is bottled God.

DYLAN THOMAS

I'd like to believe in heaven, not least because I'd like to meet my mum and dad again, to find out whether the Welsh dresser was meant to go to me or my brother.

JOHN PEEL

My feelings towards Christ are that he was a bloody good bloke even though he wasn't as funny as Margaret Thatcher.

TERRY JONES

Must that silly old sod travel quite so much? He must cost each country he visits a bloody fortune. All for an idiot who says it's a sin for a man to lust after his own wife.

RICHARD BURTON *on the Pope*

Why not both?

RICHARD BURTON *after being asked if he wanted to be a good actor or a household name*

May I congratulate you on being the only man in your team?

JAMES CALLAGHAN *to Margaret Thatcher. Thatcher is alleged to have replied, 'That's one more than you've got in yours'*

Harold Macmillan once asked me to say something to make him laugh. 'The Liberal Party', I said.

HARRY SECOMBE

Who's in a hurry?

ROBERT BENCHLEY *after being informed that alcohol was 'slow poison'*

I said to the waiter, 'The chicken I've got here is cold'. He said, 'It ought to be. It's been dead two weeks'.

TOMMY COOPER

As far as the sun.

RAY REARDON *when asked by an optician how far he could see*

Capital punishment.

DYLAN THOMAS *on being asked to describe a trip to London*

I give up – what good is it?

TOMMY COOPER *after being asked if he knew what 'good clean fun' was*

Not while I'm alive he isn't.

ERNEST BEVIN *after being asked if he thought Aneurin Bevan was his own worst enemy*

I wouldn't kiss her under anaesthetic.

DAI JONES, Llanilar, *when he was asked if he would kiss a certain lady 'under the mistletoe'*

When interviewers ask me what I love most about life I always say 'Life itself'.

KATHERINE JENKINS

He asked me if I'd lived here all my life. 'Not yet' I told him.

LEE EVANS

I said to the doctor, 'How do I stand?' He said, 'That's what puzzles me!'

TOMMY COOPER

He would, wouldn't he?

MANDY RICE-DAVIES *after being informed that Lord Astor had denied her allegations of improper behaviour during the Profumo scandal in 1963*

For me the problem is seeing more of a certain small-minded female on the box.

JANET STREET-PORTER *when she was asked what she thought of Anne Robinson's TV show* What's the Problem?

He's never been on my party list anyway.

RICHARD BURTON *on the Pope when the Vatican publicly denounced his extra-marital affair with Liz Taylor in 1962*

Clark Gable was one of the nicest men I ever met. He rang me up when I came to Hollywood. I didn't believe it was him on the line. 'If that's Clark Gable,' I said, 'this is Norman Shearer.'

TOMMY FARR

A Welsh sheep farmer was having a driving lesson. 'Now Mr Evans,' said the instructor, 'can you make a U-Turn? 'No,' replied the farmer, 'but I can make its eyes water.'

BILL SHIPTON

And they said it wouldn't last.

RICHARD BURTON *after coming back from his honeymoon with Liz Taylor*

Not very.

DYLAN THOMAS *to a man who refused to admit him to his house because he said he was 'entertaining' at the time*

A man went to the doctor with a strawberry growing out of his head. The doctor said, 'I'll give you some cream for that'.

TOMMY COOPER

No. I miss the chauffeur.

RACHEL ROBERTS *after being asked by Jill Bennett if she missed her chauffeur-driven car when her career slumped*

It depends on what time of the day it is.

ALAN RICKMAN *when asked what kind of person he was*

It's a pity that people have to leave theirs on Goose Green in order to prove it.

NEIL KINNOCK *after being asked if he thought that Margaret Thatcher had 'guts'*

Many happy returns.

T.E. LAWRENCE *to a colonel who said to him, 'I'm 92 today – what do you say to that?'*

When I first got to Italy, people asked me if I thought I was going to have trouble understanding a foreign language. 'How could I?' I told them, 'I once worked with Kenny Dalglish!'

IAN RUSH

REVULSION

The Europa Press belongs to George Reavey, that sandy, bandy, lock-jawed, French-lettered, VD'd, mock-barmy, smarmy, chance-his-army tick of a piddling crook who lives in his own armpit.

DYLAN THOMAS

Frankly, I hate bloody gadgets.

DESMOND LLEWELYN, *gadget man extraordinaire*

Many people remember Richard Burton as a great Shakespearean actor with a deep commanding voice. I remember him as a coarse, mean drunk.

EDDIE FISHER

I hate interviews. It's hard to sound enthusiastic when you're asked the same question 50 times a day.

CHARLOTTE CHURCH

I've never played Romeo; it's beyond my capacity. The urge to kiss somebody on the stage is beyond me. I can't bear to be touched either on stage or screen. It has to be very carefully arranged. That's why I prefer to act with my wife more than any other woman in the world.

RICHARD BURTON

Not since Caligula made his horse a senator has there been such a ridiculous appointment.

JOHN MORRIS *after William Hague became Secretary of State for Wales in 1995*

Conservatives travel best in gangs, hanging around like bunches of bananas, thick-skinned and yellow.

NEIL KINNOCK

There's only one line in all of Tennessee Williams' plays I consider memorable: a stage direction in *A Streetcar Named Desire*.

RICHARD BURTON

Most moviegoers are sick to death of the dingy sexpot who lives next door and the hairy oaf who's screwing her.

RAY MILLAND

Directors don't want a manager who's enterprising, experienced and strong-willed. They want a yes-man, a mealy-mouthed prop for boardroom ego, a creeper who's prepared to carry the can without complaining.

TREVOR FORD

We exist in a condition of almost permanent stupidity.

DIC EDWARDS *on mankind*

I never liked the way Richard Burton cultivated the Olivier mannerisms – the sudden fortissimos, the instant access to the emotions and all the characteristics of the shouting school of acting.

ALAN BENNETT

University students love Caradoc Evans, and pelt him with stones whenever he goes out.

DYLAN THOMAS

Where journalists are concerned, there's no word so derogatively stinking [that] sums up the congested stink of their constipation.

CAITLIN THOMAS

Every now and then someone will say to me in a condemnatory fashion, 'Tommy Cooper never felt the need to tell smutty jokes'. 'No,' I always reply. 'But he did feel the need to drink a bottle of scotch a day, beat up his wife and have a long-term affair with his wardrobe assistant. If he gave his wife the choice, I reckon she'd have preferred a blue joke to a black eye.'

FRANK SKINNER

I hated the Sixties. To me they were one long wet Wednesday afternoon on the Waterloo Road.

ANTHONY HOPKINS

RUGBY

I would argue that through my newspaper column and broadcasting with the BBC I've made a bigger contribution to rugby than most coaches in tracksuits.

BARRY JOHN

Rugby, as played by the Welsh, is not a game. It is a tribal mystery.

GWYN THOMAS

Two men are talking in a pub. One of them says, 'As far as I'm concerned, Wales is nothing but a country of streetwalkers and rugby players.' 'Oi' the other interjects, 'my mother is Welsh.' 'Really,' the first man says, 'what position does she play?'

DAVE ALLEN

When the opponent is England, it is war.

TREVOR FISHLOCK

Before our five-a-side in training one day Barry John yelled, 'Let's have Wales versus The Rest'. Someone shouted, 'But you're the only Welshman here'. He said, 'Yeah, me against you f***ing lot'. That's him.

TERRY WESTLEY

I would give up everything I've ever achieved in acting to have played rugby for Wales. If we beat England at Twickenham, I'd die happy.

RICHARD BURTON

I was a bigger hero in Italy than I was in Wales, maybe because Wales is a rugby union nation.

JOHN CHARLES

A real Welshman doesn't care who does it as long as someone beats England.

GREN JONES

Did Llanelli create Phil Bennett or was it Phil Bennett that created Llanelli?

IDRIS REYNOLDS

I got on really well with Brian O'Driscoll on the Lions tour but he's a very different character to me off the field. I've never really been able to get my head around it. I'm still shocked by someone who wants to rip my head off, call me every name under the sun in a blind rage for 80 minutes, and then buy me a drink afterwards.

GAVIN HENSON

I remember seeing the great Colin Meads in action at St Helens for the first time and being amazed that he wasn't ten feet tall, with one eye in the middle of his forehead.

GARETH EDWARDS

I remember when J.P.R. Williams gathered an awkward rolling ball against Scotland in 1976 and the Scottish wing raced up to tackle him. A voice shouted from the ground, 'Worry him! Worry him!' A well-oiled Welsh voice replied from the bowels of the North Enclosure, 'Tell him his mother's ill.'

MAX BOYCE

People often wonder where the famous Welsh sidestep came from. I'll tell you. On the pavements in the Rhondda that was the way you avoided the crowds and the lamp-posts. And if you found yourself on the road it was simply the way you avoided the traffic. It was essential for survival.

CLIFF JONES

I like to get in one really good tackle early on in a game – even if it's late.

RAY GRAVELL

Worryfield.

CLEM THOMAS's *description of Murrayfield, the Welsh nemesis*

I once saw Ray McLoughlin handle a Waikato prop in New Zealand as if he was a piece of inanimate substance to be shifted up and down on a car jack.

GARETH EDWARDS

The one-handed palmer can always reach higher, they say. They may be right but the result is that nearly every line-out is like a tropical island – all waving palms.

VIVIAN JENKINS

Many players are called internationals today only because you have to have 15 players on the pitch.

BARRY JOHN

I gave up playing rugby when the competition decided they'd rather kick me than the ball. Any moron can kick a ball but how many can say they've kicked the crap out of a famous film star's head?

RICHARD BURTON

We may not beat the All Blacks too often but at least we usually come second.

HUW ELLIS

The only real amateur in my book is the one who pays his own expenses.

VIVIAN JENKINS

There was an atheist in Cardiff that needed converting so they took him to the rugby ground and kicked him through the posts.

MAX BOYCE

It greatly saddens us old-timers to see cricket scores being rattled up against Wales, to witness people leaving stadiums with glum faces. I believe the referee even blew up early once to spare us further torture.

BARRY JOHN

A major rugby tour by the British Isles to New Zealand is a cross between a medieval crusade and a prep school outing.

JOHN HOPKINS

The job of Welsh coach is like a minor part in a Quentin Tarantino film. You stagger on, hallucinate, nobody seems to understand a word you say, you throw up, and then you get shot.

MARK REASON

Rugby is ballet, opera, dance – and then sheer bloody murder.

RICHARD BURTON

I have an immediate shudder if I blaspheme. I do a lot of shuddering on the rugby field.

GARETH EDWARDS

My mother was up there in the stand. She doesn't know a bugger about rugby but she knows we won.

DELME THOMAS *after an unlikely victory*

Rugby was a game which evolved in the small communities clustered around the pitheads. It has been enriched by the deadly rivalries between the villages. A young man pulling on the shirt of his home team is fighting for his dad, his mam, his auntie, his uncle, his granny, his kid brother, Mrs Lewis next door and Mr Jones the Bread.

TREVOR FISHLOCK

Richard Burton's father had one last order: that if his funeral coincided with one of Aberavon's home matches it was to be postponed.

FERGUS CASHIN

Will Gareth Thomas ever make a captain? The short answer's no. And the long answer's no as well.

GRAHAM HENRY

There was a period in the rugby history of Wales when any season containing a victory over England was judged a success even if all the other matches were lost.

DAVID ROBBINS

If Wales don't score again I'll be canonised.

J.C. DALY *after scoring a late try against the Welsh in 1948 and thereby winning the Triple Crown for Ireland*

How can you put a £5 referee in charge of a £20,000 competition?

Former Cardiff coach **ALUN EVANS** *after a Welsh defeat in 1993*

If you broke Gareth Chilcott's arm he'd kick you. If you broke his leg he'd bite you. And if you took all his teeth out he'd head butt you.

NICK FARR-JONES

Truth is a shadowy wing-three-quarter running forever down a ghostly touchline without anyone ever catching him.

MEREDITH JONES

Losing at Twickenham is more than coming second in a rugby match. It is a national disaster.

GARETH EDWARDS

The Welsh rugby team call me their weapon of 'mass distraction'.

KATHERINE JENKINS

SARCASM

I went to buy a Hoover and was offered one with 'varying degrees of suction'. I ask you! Did you ever use a Hoover that wasn't at the top suction level? Are we supposed to look at the dirt on the carpet and say, 'Aye aye, let's just have the top bit off, I like the rest!'

RHOD GILBERT

We are assured that a shark's bite is painless. When the jaws make their big play for me I shall remember this and feel consoled.

GWYN THOMAS

Wasn't it Winston Churchill who always fired his underlings by letter? Who would have thought the old man to have had so much milk in him?

RICHARD BURTON

A friend once gave me a present of a teddy bear holding a gun. I think he was trying to tell me I was schizoid.

ANTHONY HOPKINS

I'm playing so bad these days even Stephen Hendry is capable of beating me.

MARK WILLIAMS *during a poor spell in his career*

Vinnie Jones admits he threw a piece of toast at Gary Lineker. What he didn't say was that it was still in the toaster.

TONY BANKS

I read the newspapers avidly. It is my one form of continuous fiction.

ANEURIN BEVAN

Paul Merton is an alien from Planet Stroppy.

IAN HISLOP

You're growing on me – like a rash.

HELEN ADAMS *to Paul Howard in* Big Brother 2

When I'd played 15 first team games for United, I knocked on the gaffer's door, went in and told him I thought I deserved a club car. He shouted, 'Club car? Club bike, more like.' I haven't been in there since.

RYAN GIGGS *on Alex Ferguson in 2002*

She couldn't edit a bus ticket.

KELVIN MACKENZIE *on Janet Street-Porter after she was appointed editor of* Independent on Sunday *in 1999*

Poor Richard Jenkins – snap!

RACHEL ROBERTS's *elegy to another tortured soul – Richard Burton – in a journal entry*

Viewed as drama, World War I was somewhat disappointing.

D.W. GRIFFITH

If he hid in a quarry he'd put red flags all around it.

GEORGE BERNARD SHAW *on T.E. Lawrence*

Oliver Goldsmith wasn't a very good doctor. He was advised to give up medicine on the grounds that if he were resolved to kill, he should concentrate on his enemies.

DANNIE ABSE

My Barbie Is A Crack Whore.

Message emblazoned on **CHARLOTTE CHURCH**'s *T-shirt*

Philosophers before Kant had a tremendous advantage over philosophers after Kant in that they didn't have to waste time studying Kant.

BERTRAND RUSSELL

The choir grouped itself and sang something ineffably sad. At least three members looked ready for martyrdom.

H.V. MORTON

It was a quiet affair – just Dian's family and mine, most of the population of her home town, and press and television cameras.

MICHAEL ASPEL *on marrying a Welsh wife*

Charlotte has a great voice. It's her mouth that's the problem.

GEORGE JOHNSON *on Charlotte Church. (She used to date his son, Steven.)*

An Italian player once asked me of English training, 'Are they trying to produce cross-country runners or all-in wrestlers?'

JOHN CHARLES

Playing a British spy dressed up as a German officer, Richard Burton added to the confusion by sporting a pageboy hairstyle and giving his usual impersonation of a Welsh rugby forward who has just been told that he has been dropped from the team.

CLIVE JAMES *on Burton in* Where Eagles Dare

Danny Blanchflower was a lovely lad even though he was Irish.

JOHN CHARLES

I presume we'll be having a finger buffet.

ANTHONY HOPKINS *to Bill Clinton when he was invited to the White House after playing 'Hannibal the cannibal' in* The Silence of the Lambs

There are quite a few directors who couldn't organise a Sunday school raffle.

TREVOR FORD

A tourist stopped to chat with a Cardi farmer who was putting up a building. 'What is it?' he asked. 'If I can let it,' said the farmer, 'it's a rustic cottage. And if I can't, it's a cow shed.'

CHRISTIE DAVIES

Winston Churchill talks like somebody from the 18th century, not the 20th. His only answer to a difficult situation is to get a gun boat.

ANEURIN BEVAN

We Europeans did our best to help America win the Ryder Cup in 2006. We picked Ian Woosnam as captain.

OLIVER HOLT

I saw *Under Milk Wood* on television and I thought the best thing in the programme was the 20 minute breakdown.

GEORGE MURRAY

'See Naples and die' is a famous Italian proverb. I have a different one: spend a year with Juventus and die a thousand times.

IAN RUSH

Blessed is the man who, having nothing to say, abstains from giving us evidence of the fact.

GEORGE ELIOT

For those wretched souls unable to watch *Big Brother* all day, here's what you missed: Maggot's fry-up, live coverage of which was so excessive I had time to count 94 beans on his plate.

JOHN PERRY

Blessed are the war-makers. Theirs is the kingdom of heaven.

HUW WHELDON

Augustus John was a terrifying driver. I don't think he used the gears or clutch at all. He just went zooming along at enormous speed. He ran over one of his own sons once and killed him but as he had so many it didn't seem to touch him very much.

CAITLIN THOMAS

SELF-CRITICISM

I was once inveigled into a remake of *The Awful Truth*, which turned out to be a fizzle of the worst kind, and for which I still haven't paid. And rightly so.

RAY MILLAND

Faustus is one play I don't have to do any work on. I *am* Faustus.

RICHARD BURTON

I am the drunkest man in the world.

DYLAN THOMAS

Other than when playing darts, I become confused at the mere mention of figures.

NEIL KINNOCK

I was always my own severest critic. It was the only way to improve.

JOHN CHARLES

My life has been one long meeting. Even on the few committees I don't yet belong to, the agenda winks at me when I pass.

GWYN THOMAS

I've got so many shells I've forgotten what the pea looks like.

DAVID BOWIE

I shall always be more or less suspect.

AUGUSTUS JOHN

I'm the most inauthentic writer in Wales – hopefully.

EDWARD THOMAS

I've always felt very strange on this bloody planet. It's like I've got a gene missing. I have this notion there was some special book they passed out at birth and I missed it.

ANTHONY HOPKINS

Nothing grows in our garden except washing: And babies.

DYLAN THOMAS

People say Tiger Woods spends three hours in the gym every day of his life. I'm sure I haven't spent three hours in the gym on *any* day of my life.

IAN WOOSNAM

One, I am a Welshman. Two, I am a drunkard. Three, I am a lover of the human race, especially women.

DYLAN THOMAS *when asked to describe himself*

I am employed mainly in accepting invitations and getting out of keeping them.

AUGUSTUS JOHN

After I saw *Who's Afraid of Virginia Woolf?* I wanted to kill myself because I thought I was so indifferent.

RICHARD BURTON

I'm just a broad. I didn't know I was destroying a great actor.

LIZ TAYLOR *after the decline of Richard Burton*

I have no message whatsoever. I really have nothing to say.

DAVID BOWIE

We have exchanged our countrymen, our farms and our smallholdings for the industrial Mammon and the cheap bread.

DAVID JAMES JONES

The main reason I laugh at my jokes is out of bewilderment. I can't believe I'm getting away with such dreadful material.

TOMMY COOPER

My life has been a preparation for something that never happened.

SAUNDERS LEWIS

I hardly ever listen to a manager in the dressing-room.

NEVILLE SOUTHALL

I'm the kind of ham who wants to rush into every scene and chew the scenery.

RICHARD BURTON

I look like a heifer on TV.

CHARLOTTE CHURCH

My self-esteem is so bad, when I'm in bed with my boyfriend I fantasise that I'm someone else.

MYFANWY EDWARDS

I am not, to my unlimited sorrow, a spontaneous person, not since my halcyon Isadora Duncan days when I chose to fancy myself as flowing with melody, movement and everything but the kitchen sink.

CAITLIN THOMAS

My memory's going. I cut myself shaving this morning and forgot to bleed.

TOMMY COOPER

I'm just a poor schmuck from the Welsh hills.

DAVID MCCALLUM

I'm an addictive personality. I used to be addicted to alcohol. Now I'm addicted to Alcoholics Anonymous.

ANTHONY HOPKINS

I'm odd. Don't imagine the great-jawed writer brooding over his latest masterpiece in the oak study but rather a curly little person smoking too many cigarettes with a crocked lung, and writing his vague verses in the back room of a provincial villa.

DYLAN THOMAS

I'd like to thank my parents for making me the person I am today. I do forgive you.

CATHERINE ZETA-JONES *at the Tony Awards in June 2010*

For some time I was very promising. Then I entered my decadence. There was a fortnight or so in which I was all right but I missed it. I think I was abroad.

EMLYN WILLIAMS

SEX

So another feather-brained hoofer finds it impossible to keep his trousers up for more than five minutes. Big swinging mickey. Do you know what would be a *real* story? If one of those head-the-balls had a night in at home. I can see the headlines next week: 'Top Footballer in Steamy Romps with Wife Shock – Star Bedded his Own Missus!'

MICK THE MAVERICK *on Ryan Giggs's bed-hopping antics*

I can't sing a song that isn't sexy unless I'm in church doing a hymn.

TOM JONES

Unless you've got a bit of earth, mud and sex in you, there's no heart really.

DAWN FRENCH

Evelyn Waugh famously said, 'All this fuss about sleeping together. For physical pleasure I'd sooner go to the dentist any day.' Well in my part of Wales it's now easier to find someone to sleep with than it is to find a dentist.

PATRICK HANNAN

After a man has sex with a woman he thinks he has a hold on her but when a woman has sex with a man she's just hoping it will happen again, that he'll come back for more.

RACHEL GRIFFITHS

As soon as you have kids you can't make noise when you're having sex in case they walk in on you. You turn into Marcel Marceau.

LEE EVANS

He discovered a massage parlour where a little Japanese lady walked up his spine.

SIÂN PHILLIPS *on Peter O'Toole in Tokyo*

Sion asked his wife if she fancied anything out of the *Kama Sutra*. Anwen said, 'No, cariad. I'm not all that keen on Indian takeaways.'

MILES JEFFREYS

I agree with Stephen Booth's irrefutable assertion that William Shakespeare was almost certainly homosexual, bisexual or heterosexual.

DANNIE ABSE

Far better than sex is the pleasure of drinking at someone else's expense.

HARRY SECOMBE

He once urinated into his pint on the Irish ferry because he said that if he used the public urinal, the head waiter would make homosexual advances.

RICHARD BOOTH *on his friend Frank Lewis*

There goes the good time that was had by all.

BETTE DAVIS *on a promiscuous starlet*

I've yet to meet anybody who can have exciting sex in Welsh.

EDWARD THOMAS

I was in bed with Caitlin ten minutes after I first met her.

DYLAN THOMAS

Richard Burton is the greatest phallic symbol in the world.

MARTIN RITT

Richard Burton wasn't prejudiced. He once told me he would screw any race, creed or colour.

VINCE CARUSO, *an RAF colleague of Burton*

World War II was at its height and a group of women were in the bread queue. Suddenly, one of them jumped the queue. 'Who do you think you are? said the woman in front of her. 'I'm Lloyd George's daughter,' came the reply. And then a chorus of voices chirped, 'So are the rest of us.'

INTERNET JOKE

A Welsh pervert is a man who'd miss a rugby international to go to bed with Catherine Zeta-Jones.

WYN JENKINS

Errol Flynn must have had the most overworked prostate gland in the business.

RAY MILLAND

I once made love on the top of Beachy Head in the black velvet dark with the seawater smashing and sucking at the cliffs below. We must have been very good because that part of the cliff has now disintegrated and fallen into the sea.

RUTH JOSEPH

You can't make a sexy man good but you can make a good man sexy.

MELANIE GLYN

What would you call a Welshman who owns goats as well as sheep? Bisexual.

DAI JENKINS

The first time I had sex was a bit of a disaster. It was a bit quick, and I threw up afterwards. It was on a hillside with sheep around us, which didn't help.

GLYN WISE

A Welshman's idea of romance is a full moon and a sleeping shepherd.

BRYAN WENTWORTH

My father told me all about the birds and the bees. The liar – I went steady with a woodpecker till I was 21.

BOB HOPE

Joan Crawford slept with every male on the MGM lot except Lassie.

BETTE DAVIS

I have a great belief in safe sex. That's why I put a safety railing round the bunk bed.

GARETH ELLIS

Celebrities don't pay prostitutes for sex. They pay them not to tell.

RUFUS SEWELL

A woman once asked me for a double entendre – so I gave her one.

DAFYDD JONES

I came out because I was going in.

IAN H. WATKINS *describing how he announced he was gay before entering the* Celebrity Big Brother *house in January 2007*

Often men who are obsessed by sex are not very good at it. Those who are very potent don't have to be obsessed. They just do it then forget about it and smoke a fag.

CAITLIN THOMAS

What's the definition of Welsh rarebit? A Cardiff virgin.

INTERNET JOKE

Dafydd: Why don't you tell me when you have an orgasm?
Heather: I would, but you're never there.

MILES JEFFREYS

Surely the sex business isn't worth all this damned fuss. I've only met a handful of people who cared a biscuit for it.

T.E. LAWRENCE

It doesn't matter who I go to bed with because they're all really Caitlin.

DYLAN THOMAS

To the Irish nuns at my south Wales convent, sex was a concept regarded as only marginally less heinous than Communism.

VRON GREGG

I got tits before everyone else and I wanted boys touching them right from the minute they grew.

DAWN FRENCH

Tom Jones would go to bed with anything that had a pulse, though he prefers more mature women – maybe eighteen or nineteen years old.

CHRIS ELLIS

At seventeen I was desperate to lose my virginity. It seemed like a ball and chain holding me back. I just needed to get it over and done with. It was something that needed to be ticked off so I could move on.

JANET STREET-PORTER

Her dachshund, she said, was oversexed. Could I please do something to dampen his ardour? Well indeed I could. I recommended the remedy that has dampened male ardour since time began. I found him a wife.

BUSTER LLOYD-JONES

The whole history of sex is a disgraceful pigsty of mistiming.

CAITLIN THOMAS

Am I the only person in Britain who wasn't sexually abused as a child?

VICTOR LEWIS-SMITH

Before I was 16 someone set up a website counting down the days until it was legal for me to have sex.

CHARLOTTE CHURCH

Sex on television is all right as long as you don't fall off.

EUAN GRIFFITH

Nothing costs as much as free love.

GWYN WILLIAMS

I must be the luckiest man in the world. Not only am I bisexual but I'm also Welsh.

JOHN OSBORNE

Dad told me I was the most precious thing in his life and if any randy geek laid a finger on me he would hurt them badly in their Brut-sprinkled soft places.

DAWN FRENCH

In the '60s and '70s I went through debutantes like a dose of salts.

DAI LLEWELYN

Let us remember that sex is everyone's problem. Even Aunt Edna has an itch under the tea tray.

JOHN OSBORNE

SNOOKER

Stephen Hendry is cueing like Terry Griffiths these days so he must be a genius to be able to pot a ball.

DOMINIC DALE

I would have won if he hadn't turned up.

CLIFF WILSON *after being beaten by Steve Davis in the 1988 Rothman's Grand Prix*

Steve Davis is two blacks better than the rest of the world.

DOUG MOUNTJOY *on Davis in 1981, the year he beat him in the world final*

People ask me why I don't play faster. I could. But I'd miss.

TERRY GRIFFITHS

He wasn't so much a hurricane at the end of his career as a gentle wind.

MATTHEW STEVENS *on Alex Higgins*

He played like an arse.

MARK WILLIAMS *on why he beat Stephen Hendry in the 2006 China Open*

Some of the new players like being flashy, running round the table at the rate of knots. But no matter how fast you play, you still only get one point for a red and seven for a black.

RAY REARDON

Cliff Wilson can see better with one eye than most players can with two.

JACK KARNEHM

If you wanted to paint high ceilings in Michelangelo's day it paid to know the Pope. If you wanted to be a professional snooker player just after World War II you also needed Joe Davis' papal seal of approval.

CLIVE EVERTON

I'm in the final now, you know.

> **TERRY GRIFFITHS** *uttering his famous one-liner in 1979. A few days later he was world champion*

Alex Higgins used to sit down, light a cigarette, chalk his cue, file his tip and have a drink... all in one movement. I get 50 puffs out of a cigarette. He got three.

TERRY GRIFFITHS

Steve Davis said it best: You've got to act like it means nothing when it means everything.

GEOFF THOMAS

Gentle games like snooker, bowls and croquet have hidden qualities. Seemingly sedate, even somnolent, a match can suddenly ignite. Aggressive tactics can destroy a carefully built-up advantage. Initiative can pendulum at a stroke.

DAVID RHYS-JONES

Ryan Day shakes his head up and down before he takes his shots but they still go in. If this continues they'll all be at it.

TERRY GRIFFITHS

I once played snooker in a mud hut with a thatched roof for a wealthy businessman out in the Transvaal.

RAY REARDON

I used to know someone like Barry Hearn at school. His dad was rich and he was the only boy who could afford a football. If you didn't pass it to him he would pick it up and go home.

CLIFF WILSON

I won the Grand Prix too early on in my career. I wasn't ready to be a winner. It was like: I've beaten everyone. What do I do now?

DOMINIC DALE

He could lose a world final and still look like it was a Monday morning knockabout in his local club. If he was any more laidback he'd be horizontal.

DENNIS TAYLOR *on Mark Williams*

The Crucible has been called the Theatre of Dreams. But it can also be the Theatre of Nightmares.

TERRY GRIFFITHS

It was a common complaint when Walter Lindrum, the great billiards champion, was hunched over the table making endless runs of nursery cannons, that a spectator could watch a whole session and never see his face.

CLIVE EVERTON

My nana could play better, and she's 83.

JOHN MERCER *on the 2006 World Snooker final between Graeme Dott and Peter Ebdon*

Having grown up with the idea that Llanelli was the centre of the universe, I had it confirmed when Terry Griffiths became world snooker champion.

RHODRI DAVIES

The whole idea of snooker is to make your opponent feel miserable.

CLIVE EVERTON

I'm playing Cliff Thorburn tomorrow. I'm going to bring a book.

CLIFF WILSON, *referring to Thorburn's reputation for slow play*

I'm playing Ronnie O'Sullivan next. If I play like I did against Andy Hicks in the last round I won't be able to beat *Gilbert* O'Sullivan.

MARK WILLIAMS *at the Welsh Masters in 2012*

Matthew Stevens' natural expression is that of a man who may have mislaid his winning lottery ticket.

PAUL WEAVER

Snooker is 90 per cent in the head.

DOMINIC DALE

I put a lot of store by safety. If your opponent can't see the ball he can't pot it.

RAY REARDON

Compared to what I used to do for a living, delivering letters, snooker is money for old rope.

TERRY GRIFFITHS

You can feel so low at snooker that when you come to the table you're hoping there's nothing 'on' so you don't make a fool of yourself.

CLIVE EVERTON

SPORT

When I was four years old I played chess blindfolded against ten people all at once. I lost every game.

ROBERT BENCHLEY

There are plenty of Welsh people whose prime literature is a soccer or rugby match programme.

TREVOR FISHLOCK

Did you hear about the Englishman who won five tons of manure in a crap game?

HARRY SECOMBE

It beats cockfighting for a living.

JOBY CHURCHILL *on boxing*

'Lucky Tommy Farr.' How familiar the chorus. It is nearer to the truth to say that by persistency, dog instinct and cussedness that I have escaped from the wolves in which the prize-ring abounds.

TOMMY FARR

The spectator sees more of a game than the players.

ANNA SWAN

It's tough at the top but tougher at the bottom.

DAVID VAUGHAN

You can only play as well as the opposition allow you to.

ROY PAUL

They'll never bury Ian Woosnam because they won't be able to get his heart into the coffin.

LEE TREVINO

Vinnie Jones is to fine and fair football what Count Dracula was to blood transfusions.

MICHAEL HERD

The long par-five ninth hole at Llanymynech had a huge significance for me. There was a 15-yard hollow stretching across the fairway. School work, the moon landings, England's painful 3–2 defeat against West Germany in the 1970 World Cup: nothing mattered as much as hitting my drive past that hollow.

IAN WOOSNAM

Italian contracts bind you every inch, body and soul, to the club, thereby making you the best-paid slaves in the sports industry.

JOHN CHARLES

I hear Ryan Giggs' wife is going to get half of everything if they divorce. That means she'll have more league medals than Stephen Gerrard.

DAFYDD HUMPHRIES

Clement Atlee brings to politics the tepid enthusiasm of a lazy summer afternoon at a cricket match.

ANEURIN BEVAN

Most professional golfers treat their caddies like friends. Some treat them like employees. A few treat them like children.

IAN WOOSNAM

Welsh leisure activities can be summed up very briefly: Sport, Beer and Argument.

JOHN RICHARDS

Evan Morgan broke the 100 yards record wearing mining boots. He fell down a shaft.

CHRISTIE DAVIES

STEREOTYPES

The Englishman, although he never boasts about being English, loves to hear a Scotsman bragging about Scotland or an Irishman crying about Ireland. Jock and Paddy are clear and definite characters but Taffy is more elusive. His silence is strange. No comic papers have made him loveable.

H.V. MORTON

Like the Greeks the Welsh enjoy their woes and nourish them in abundance, often preferring remembering to living.

ALUN RICHARDS

Show a Welshman a thousand doors, one of which is marked 'Self-Destruction' and that's the one he'll choose.

RICHARD BURTON

There are hardly two things more peculiarly English than Welsh rarebit and Irish stew.

G.K. CHESTERTON

The Welsh have many colourful and distinctive customs and traditions, most of which were invented by the Welsh Tourist Board.

JOHN RICHARDS

Who are the Welsh – apart from good singers?

P. BERRESFORD ELLIS

Wales has often been viewed as a region rather than a nation.

RUTH SHADE

My mother didn't think highly of women. She was a great believer in the virgin/whore dichotomy. Unmarried career women for her were unnatural, dried-up spinsters.

CERIDWEN HUGHES

To hear some people talk, one would imagine that I am a half-crazed Welsh dragon snorting down the middle of the field spitting fire and gorging myself on every defender who happens to be within eating distance.

TREVOR FORD

THEATRE

I never saw Jimmy Porter, the archetypal angry young man from *Look Back in Anger*, as especially angry. I'd seen working class anger during a lockout at a coalmine and that was a good deal more terrifying than Jimmy's bad temper.

SIÂN PHILLIPS

It out-Oliviers Olivier for the wildest Oedipal agonies.

ALASTAIR COOKE *on Richard Burton's* Hamlet

For too many people, going to the theatre is just a little bit of a nuisance. When going to have a good old laugh gets worthy, the writing is on the wall.

GRIFF RHYS JONES

He's miscast and she's Miss Taylor.

EMLYN WILLIAMS *on Richard Burton and Liz Taylor in* Private Lives

Ivor Novello plays the king with all the assurance of a man who has gauged public taste down to the last emotional millimetre.

MILTON SHULMAN *reviewing* King's Rhapsody *in 1949*

I've always had the theatre in my veins but I'd prefer blood.

PHILIP MADOC

Rex Harrison once told me that when he started in the theatre, actors had to ape gentlemen. If one had a working class accent he was confined to playing servants or members of the lower order.

ELIZABETH HARRISON

Wales is the only country in the world where television came before theatre.

WILBERT LLOYD ROBERTS

Ninety per cent of film directors have been terrific to me but the theatre is a breeding ground for fabulous bullshit.

ANTHONY HOPKINS

I saw the play under adverse conditions. The curtain was up.

ROBERT BENCHLEY

In films you get the money, in theatre the applause.

DONALD HOUSTON

Anyone who attempts to play *Hamlet* has to be a lunatic.

ALAN RICKMAN

If ever I'm in a town with only two theatres and one is playing *A Doll's House* and the other *The Pirates of Penzance*, you'll find me at the latter.

RAY MILLAND

My lack of height came against me more in the theatre than anywhere else. On television and in movies it's not so bad. Midgets like Al Pacino can still get the big roles.

DAVID JASON

No matter how good a play or an operetta may seem to be, if it fails to dram an audience then to my mind it ceases to exist.

IVOR NOVELLO

I lift my hat to Mr Novello. He can wade through tosh with the straightest face: the tongue never visibly approaches the cheek.

A left-handed compliment to **NOVELLO** *after he appeared in* Glamorous Night *in 1935*

The old cliché that the French theatre is a writer's theatre, the British theatre is an actor's theatre and the American theatre is a director's theatre – I don't believe any of that. The theatre is essentially a writer's theatre and directors are relatively unimportant. They're no more than jumped-up stage managers.

RICHARD BURTON

The process of casting a play in Ireland began with the question, 'Is he all right?' The phrase 'All right' meant 'Back in circulation after a spell in hospital, drying out'.

SIÂN PHILLIPS

A Welsh actor with a fondness for 'Method' improvisation was annoying the man who wrote the play in which he was performing. On the day before the first show he reassured the playwright by saying, 'Don't worry, I know my lines now'. 'Yes,' replied the playwright, 'but do you know *my* ones?'

CARWYN WEBB

Theatre in Wales is in the doldrums. I can count on one hand the companies I would get out of bed to see.

DAVID ADAMS

How can any theatre in Wales claim to be reflecting a Welsh culture when it refuses to use the playwrights of Wales?

DIC EDWARDS

The reason I still appear on stage is because I've always been afraid of audiences and I want to conquer that.

RICHARD BURTON

This cocky genial fellow sweats apprehensively and occasionally bellows, but frequently gives the impression that he is a Rotarian pork butcher about to tell the stalls a dirty story.

FELIX BARKER *on Anthony Hopkins in* Macbeth *in 1973*

Notice outside London theatre: 'The part of the Welshman has been filled. The Dai is cast.'

CHRISTIE DAVIES

Drama is more like a juice than a scent. A juice is held in a shape: the apple, the orange. A scent pervades.

EDWARD BOND

It's harder to act in theatre than in the movies. There's no big close-up waiting to help you when you falter. If you choose a bad film you can take the money and run, but choose a bad play and you're faced with a nightly parade of humiliation.

RICHARD BURTON

My dear Hamlet, may I use your lavatory?

WINSTON CHURCHILL *to Burton backstage at the Old Vic after he'd played his most famous stage role*

Shakespeare is a bloody nightmare. I'd prefer to be in Malibu. You're doing what 15,000 actors have done before you. Stratford-on-Avon should be knocked down and paved over.

ANTHONY HOPKINS

I was never a very good actor. A man phoned the theatre one night and asked me what time the play started. 'What time can you make it?' I replied.

HUW WATKINS

I wrote *Jackie the Jumper* because I wanted a play that would paint the full face of sensuality, rebellion and revivalism. In south Wales these three phenomena have played second fiddle only to the rugby union, which is a distillation of all three.

GWYN THOMAS

DYLAN THOMAS ON POETRY

The world is never the same once a good poem has been added to it.

Magic in a poem is always accidental.

The Welsh have written exceedingly good poetry in English. I like to think that is because they were good poets rather than good Welshmen.

Too many of the artists of Wales spend too much time talking about the position of the artists of Wales. There is only one position for an artist anywhere: upright.

Writing poetry is an incurable disease.

I am not interested in poetry. I am only interested in poems.

Poetry should be as orgiastic and organic as copulation.

TRAVEL

When my friends and I travelled to Austria we possessed only four phrases of German: 'Where is?', 'How much?', 'Where is the youth hostel?' and 'Where is the cinema?' We had our priorities right.

HUGH LOUDON

The local area was our world. If my parents travelled ten miles on the bus, that was considered a long journey.

JOHN CHARLES

Pwll: 'So you're not going to Venice this year?' Twm: 'No, it's Vienna we're not going to. It was Venice we didn't go to last year.'

WYNFORD JONES

I went to America to continue my lifelong quest for naked women in wet mackintoshes.

DYLAN THOMAS

I think I spent more time in Italy on the phone home than I did in training.

IAN RUSH *on the 'hiraeth' he experienced during his stint with Juventus*

The traffic jams in Gower are so famous, people arrive in hundreds in their cars just to see them.

GREN JONES

If a Roman colonial official of the second century could travel in Snowdonia he would recognise the hill-men of today as the tribal Britons of yesterday.

H.V. MORTON

Life can take you anywhere you want to go until you get there.

CAROLE MORGAN HOPKIN

Burton and Taylor travel down to hell on a moving staircase, a journey enlivened by the writhing of intertwined torsos, at whom Mr Burton glances as if they were corset advertisements on the London underground.

TIME *magazine on* Dr Faustus *in 1967*

Motoring is a fearfully wrong way of seeing the country but an awfully nice way of doing without railway trains.

AUGUSTUS JOHN

We even had to bring soap and a towel for having a bath.

JOHN CHARLES *on travelling abroad with the Welsh football team in the 1950s*

I love travel. I've been to almost as many places as my luggage.

BOB HOPE

I always sit on the tail end of a plane. You never hear of a plane backing into a mountain.

TOMMY COOPER

Anyone who's been abroad will know that for the rest of the world Wales hardly exists.

NIGEL JENKINS

Outside the home the motorcar was second only to the contraceptive pill in its impact on Welsh society.

CHRIS WILLIAMS

Don't rush. The sooner you fall behind, the more time you have to catch up.

ROY NOBLE

Catherine Zeta-Jones once hired a private jet to fly from Los Angeles to an awards ceremony in New York because smoking was banned on major airlines.

FIONA CUMMINS

I jumped in a taxi the other day. I said, 'King Arthur's Close'. The driver said, 'Don't worry, I'll lose him at the next set of lights.'

TOMMY COOPER

He had his driving licence taken away for life in Ireland. This was quite a remarkable feat since the highway code is not the most zealously observed piece of legislation in Limerick. However, they couldn't overlook the fact that he had managed to drive his car into a corporation bus. Twice.

ELIZABETH HARRISON *on Richard Harris, her first husband*

Riding a moped is like being on a hairdryer. Dogs are walking faster than you're going.

EDDIE IZZARD

Somebody complimented me on my driving today. They left a little note on the windscreen saying 'Parking Fine'.

TOMMY COOPER

When I was younger I used to be afraid of flying. These days I'm only afraid of crashing.

MAY BOYCE

I was in Margate last year for the summer season. A friend of mine said it was good for rheumatism so I went there and got it.

TOMMY COOPER

'Abroad' – that large home of ruined reputations.

GEORGE ELIOT

The journey from Carmarthen to Aberystwyth by train is one of the most reposeful stretches of railed track on earth. The railway company has a contract with the bees. They don't molest the passengers or try to scrounge free rides. The trains in return do not disturb the pollen.

GWYN THOMAS

With a drink or two taken he liked to travel lying on the floor of the limo with his feet out of the window.

SIÂN PHILLIPS *on Montgomery Clift*

Anthony Hopkins once told me he got into his car, drove 1,000 miles for no reason, turned the car round and then drove home again.

JAMES IVORY

THE VALLEYS

The spirit of the Valleys has been badly bruised and beaten by a bigoted, heartless government too far away to care. Today when a man is sacked for defending a principle his desperate friend or brother is glad to take his place.

MAGGIE PRYCE JONES

If a Valley person went into an English shop and said, 'You haven't got any milk, have you?' a justified response to this question would be, 'Why, don't you want any?'

DAVID JANDRELL

An American walked into a Valley bar and was asked where he was from. 'The greatest country in the world,' he replied. 'Really?' said his interrogator, 'You have a damn strange accent for a Welshman'.

IAN EVANS

Did you hear about the intellectual from the Rhondda Valley? He was ignorant in two different languages.

GWYN DAVIES

The only people who were making money were the undertakers.

BEATRICE WOOD *on life in the Valleys during World War II*

Confined and snug in its Valley, Merthyr was a community united in hardship but satisfied with its lot. You got what you expected and left disillusionment to those who dared to dream.

ANNA SWAN

The Valleys provided Wales with its own America. The Great Valleys Dream – socialism if you like – was no less potent than the Great American Dream. They both belonged to a frontier of villages suddenly upgraded into sprawling conurbations on the edge of a wilderness.

TONY CONRAN

The smells of wintergreen oil, dubbin' on the ball, beer out of enamel jugs and fish and chips are the Saturday smells of a Welsh Valley upbringing.

GARETH EDWARDS

West Wales breeds the fly-halves and the Gwent Valleys produce the mighty forwards.

CARWYN JONES

I never used to regard myself as a politician, but rather a projectile discharged from the Welsh Valleys.

ANEURIN BEVAN

VIOLENCE

We're drowning our youngsters in violence, cynicism and sadism, pumped into the living-room and even the nursery. The grandchildren of the kids who used to weep because the Little Match Girl froze to death now feel cheated if she isn't slugged, raped and thrown into a Bessemer converter.

JENKIN LLOYD JONES

Poetry readings can be dangerous in the US. I have not heard of any poet on the circuit being shot in Britain, though not a few, perhaps, deserve to be.

DANNIE ABSE

They say 'Guns don't kill people – people kill people'. Well I think the gun helps. If you just stood there and yelled 'Bang!' I don't think you'd kill too many people.

EDDIE IZZARD

If violence on TV causes violence on the streets why doesn't comedy on TV cause comedy on the streets?

DICK CAVETT

The best time I ever had with Joan Crawford was when I pushed her down the stairs in *What Ever Happened to Baby Jane?*.

BETTE DAVIS

Isn't life awful? Last week I hit Caitlin with a plate of beetroot and I'm still bleeding.

DYLAN THOMAS

Patriotism is the willingness to kill and be killed for trivial reasons.

BERTRAND RUSSELL

If you would like to hear the dangerous sounds of teeth being ground, and the creak of skin stretching as fists clench, go into a bar in the Rhondda or the Rhymney, drink someone's pint and suggest that only Welsh-speakers are Welsh.

TREVOR FISHLOCK

When I rowed with Dylan I would throw myself at him, push him to the floor, grab him by the hair and keep banging his head against it, beating the Jesus out of him. I could never kick him in the balls, though, because they're precious.

CAITLIN THOMAS

WALES

Any fool can be a crown bard of Wales because genius is low in Wales.

DAVID EMRYS JAMES

The most common crime in Wales is ram-raiding.

JIMMY CARR

These days Wales is a teeming hive of activity. Then on Sunday night everyone gets into their Volvos and goes back to the South East again.

BILL SHIPTON

Wales is a beautiful mother but she can be a dangerously possessive wife.

RHYS DAVIES

There are parts of Wales where the only concession to gaiety is a striped shroud.

GWYN THOMAS

The astonishing thing about the history of Wales is that it can be written at all.

WYNFORD VAUGHAN-THOMAS

When I imagine Wales it is always as a peopled landscape, perky with life, jumbled, intensively noisy and, in any ultimate sense, uncontrollable.

DAI SMITH

There is no decadence in Wales. There are rogues and ogres, true, but the Celtic simplicity and wonder lies over all.

RHYS DAVIES

One of the essentials we have been slow to learn in Wales, it seems to me, is that of looking at things as they are.

W.J. GRUFFYDD

I went to Wales once but it was closed.

BOB MONKHOUSE

This bloody land is full of Welshmen.

DYLAN THOMAS

The main purpose of Wales is to keep the English and Irish apart.

M.K. BISSMIRE

It's said on the quiet that Wales has always been run by women.

ANNA SNOW

It would be a great blessing for Wales if some Welshman did something for his nation that caused him to be put in prison.

SAUNDERS LEWIS

The strength of the common man was always the strength of Wales.

KEIDRYCH RHYS

To say that Wales is a nation and not a state is to emphasise the fact that it remains a soul without a body.

GWILYM DAVIES

When you come from Wales you're a f★★★ing man. We take pit ponies and put a bit of rubber hose pipe in their mouth and drag them into the sea to wash the grime off them. We're tough in Wales.

RICHARD BURTON

The land of my fathers. My fathers can have it.

DYLAN THOMAS

Not everyone in Wales looks benignly on cultural pursuits. There is a suspicion of art's loftier reaches. I am reminded of the Swansea councillor who snorted, 'Ballet? Ballet is just a leg show for the nobs!'

TREVOR FISHLOCK

When she called him a Welsh bastard he was offended but he didn't say which of the two words hurt him most.

JOE O'GORMAN

Would anyone notice if Wales disappeared, except for people in the West Country, who would then own seaside homes?

PAT FITZPATRICK

It kind of spat me out.

JOHN CALE

To live in Wales is to be mumbled at by reincarnations of Dylan Thomas in numerous diverse disguises.

PETER FINCH

Wales is forever associated with inedible salad.

GRIFF RHYS JONES

Wales is a Third World country.

PAUL McCARTNEY

There's a certain darkness in the Welsh character that's good for creating art.

ROB BRYDON

In Wales every single south or westerly facing escarpment is being smothered in wind farms. Giant tubular bird mincers whirl and moan 24 hours a day. Eventually, after a year or so, they produce just enough energy to light up Mrs Llewelyn's bedside lamp.

JEREMY CLARKSON

The definition of confusion is a Welshman being refused Irish coffee in an Indian restaurant.

DUDLEY MOORE

WEATHER

There's something in our weather that is hostile to treats, feasts and outings.

GWYN THOMAS

It was so cold, even the politicians were walking around with their hands in their pockets.

BOB HOPE

Don't knock the weather. Without it, nine out of ten people couldn't start a conversation.

ROY NOBLE

September is a strange time of the year, when the buildings stubbornly hold on to the summer heat from the odd coldish day attempting to drag it out of them.

SIÂN MELANGELL DAFYDD

My ideal of life is two people struggling against a gale, their hair blown back, sand in their eyes, and the blood tingling.

SAUNDERS LEWIS

It was so cold in Swansea last week the local flasher was spotted describing himself to a group of women.

GWEN ELLIS

The weather in Wales is subhuman and antihuman. It leads to neurosis, melancholia, and probably schizophrenia.

MARTHA GELLHORN

WEIGHT

If I'd been around when Rubens was painting I would have been revered as a fabulous model. Kate Moss? Well she would have been the paintbrush.

DAWN FRENCH

I lose an average of six pounds per performance.

TOM JONES *during his heyday*

My girlfriend was trying on a dress. 'Does my bum look big in this?' she asked me. I said, 'Why would you want your bum to look big?' She said, 'No, I want a dress to make it look smaller'. 'Oh,' I said, 'you're looking for a magic dress then.'

RHOD GILBERT

I have a weight of 20 stone squeezed into a five foot eight inch frame as a result of having been hit by a lift.

HARRY SECOMBE

In the divorce court women complain of losing weight. Outside the divorce court they complain of putting it on.

SIR ARTHUR DAVIES

Cher never diets or exercises. She stays in shape through a steady diet of vodka, Red Bull and fags.

NEW *magazine on Charlotte Church*

I went on a strict diet to look nice for my wedding. I remember looking in the mirror going, 'So *that's* what a waist looks like'.

DAWN FRENCH

I'm the only person ever to have gone to a health clinic and put *on* weight.

RACHEL ROBERTS

My slimming advice goes as follows: Eat as much as you like. Just don't swallow it.

HARRY SECOMBE

I'd rather be dead than fat.

ROALD DAHL

Big women have an abundant amount of sexual fantasies much more than thin ones. We pump more oestrogen so we want it more.

DAWN FRENCH

I'm never going to be as skinny as Posh Spice. And I hope I don't ever sing like her either.

CHARLOTTE CHURCH

Two big blokes are in a pub. One says to the other, 'Your round'. The other one says, 'So are you, you fat bastard'.

TOMMY COOPER

Fascism ordains that you have to be a certain size before you get a mortgage.

DAWN FRENCH

People like Carol Vorderman have the arrogance to think that I want a body like theirs. What I want is a body like mine. But could I have it in a smaller size, please?

ROISIN INGLE

I don't much go for the trendy dieting advice in magazines. A super-food is something you eat, a superbug is something that eats you. In the meantime, stick to a daily diet of Pringles. Sooner or later scientists are bound to declare them an excellent way of avoiding athlete's foot, and warts.

CHARLOTTE CHURCH

I used good old Guinness to put on the weight for playing Dylan Thomas in *The Edge of Love*. I enjoyed that part of the research.

MATTHEW RHYS

When I was asked to raise funds for the British Heart Foundation I realised that at eighteen and a half stone I was in danger of becoming a beneficiary of that organisation than a helper.

KEVIN JOHNS

I love food and I hate the gym. That makes for a pretty curvy combination.

CHARLOTTE CHURCH

THE WELSH

If Welsh history has one underlying theme, that theme is surely survival.

WYNFORD VAUGHAN-THOMAS

I've always found that what the Welsh don't want to see, they don't see.

CAITLIN THOMAS

The greatest gift the Welsh possess is their total absence of awe.

BRENDA MADDOX

Welsh nationalism has become the spare-time hobby of corpulent and successful men.

SAUNDERS LEWIS

The Welsh people have lived in a permanent state of emergency since about 383 AD.

GWYN WILLIAMS

Welsh artists stay in Wales too long. Giants in the dark behind the parish pump, pygmies in the nationless sun, enviously sniping at the artists of other countries rather than attempting to raise their own country's standards.

DYLAN THOMAS

The main problem of Welshness is that it isn't contagious.

LEONORA GRIFFITH

The Welsh are the same as the Irish – a lot of goddam micks and biddies, only Protestant.

JOHN FORD

The Welsh are a nation of toughs, rogues and poetic humbugs, vivid in their speech, impulsive in behaviour, and riddled with a sly and belligerent tribalism.

V.S. PRITCHETT

He was Welsh, but happily did not sing.

HUGH LEONARD

Finding out your sister is black is fine. Finding out she's Welsh is another thing entirely.

A.A. GILL

It's a scientific fact that the Great Wall of China and the Welsh sense of national outrage are the only two earthly things visible from outer space.

ANTHONY TORMEY

The Welsh, like the Irish, have a simultaneous inferiority/superiority complex. One usually turns into the other after a rugby victory, a bout of singing, or an intake of alcohol – or all three simultaneously.

DAVE ALLEN

God created the Welsh to keep the Irish and the English apart.

MICHAEL BISSMIRE

The Welsh miner is my brother; the Irish gombeen is my enemy.

CON HOULIHAN

The Welsh are born hagglers. Industrial relations are traditionally about as quick and simple as the Thirty Years War.

JOHN RICHARDS

The Irish and the Welsh are partners in crime: The Murphia and the Taffia.

WYN JENKINS

The Welsh are a brutal, shifty race who have already given our language the verb 'to welsh' as well as such ill-favoured things as the Welsh rarebit, Jack Jones, Moss Evans, and half the poisonous dwarves of the Labour Party.

AUBERON WAUGH

I love it when Welshmen tell jokes. It stops them singing for a few minutes.

BILL SHIPTON

The Welsh would have benefited from a spell of totally mindless hedonism.

GWYN THOMAS

From the earliest times the Welsh have been looked on as an unclean people. It is thus that they have preserved their racial integrity.

EVELYN WAUGH

The Welsh are the last Romans.

PETER SIMPLE

What do you call a Welshman with more than one sheep? A bigamist.

MILES JEFFREYS

In our unregenerate days we must have kept life in such an uproar. With our licentious revelry, we kept the whole of Europe awake.

GWYN THOMAS

You may never find anyone worse than a bad Welshman but you will certainly never find anyone better than a good one.

GIRALDUS CAMBRENSIS

Welshness isn't a nationality; it's a condition.

WYN GRIFFITH

Dylan Thomas was part of an extended family. Aren't all the people of Wales?

CON HOULIHAN

WORK

I can't understand people working in shops.

LAURA ASHLEY

My CV looks like I'm a job hopper but I always tell interviewers I never left any of those jobs of my own free will.

GRAHAM JONES

If the working man is the salt of the earth, the Welsh working man is that salt ground to a sharp, astringent powder.

JAMES CAMERON

I once worked in a glue factory but I left after six months. I couldn't stick it.

TOMMY COOPER

People who say that there's no point in continuing to teach Welsh on the grounds that 'It's useless' and 'Won't get you a job' are often the same people who complain when they see that it is not, and that it will.

TREVOR FISHLOCK

There's a virus which strikes down large numbers of workers every year in Wales which happens to coincide with international rugby matches. An apparently unrelated virus often carries off distant relations at exactly the same time of year, necessitating the attendance at their funerals of those workers who escaped the first virus.

JOHN RICHARDS

The House of Lords is 500 ordinary men chosen accidentally from among the unemployed.

DAVID LLOYD GEORGE

Work is easy when you have a cause. Just look at Florence Nightingale.

LAURA ASHLEY

I am not unemployed – for the reason that I have never been employed.

DYLAN THOMAS

I believe we would work out much better in the House of Commons if we did two hours digging every day.

DAVID LLOYD GEORGE

The main problem with Ireland isn't having to work hard but having to play hard.

BONNIE TYLER *after a concert in Dublin*

England is a great place to work. It's an island so the audience can't run very far.

JONATHAN PRYCE

It's easier to get a job in Hollywood than to get an agent. I eventually found one who condescended to handle me.

RAY MILLAND

I've done the most insufferable rubbish merely to have somewhere to go in the morning.

RICHARD BURTON

I have a punishing workout regimen. Every day I do three minutes on a treadmill, then I lie down, drink a glass of vodka and smoke a cigarette.

ANTHONY HOPKINS

Somebody in Hollywood once told me I couldn't be seen with a suntan because it meant I wasn't working.

MICHAEL YORK

Regular work he dodged as if it were bubonic.

GWYN THOMAS *on W.H. Davies*

I would rather live this life and die a beggar or a thief than be a working slave with no days free.

W.H. DAVIES

Trade unionists' fairytales begin with the words, 'Once upon a time and a half'.

MAX BOYCE

Why are people never too busy to tell you how busy they are?

HUW RICHARDS

In 1932 in Merthyr, life expectancy was 46. The symptoms were deprivation and disease but the cause was unemployment. It was said that a man with a job attracted sightseers.

ANNA SWAN

We expect that women will want to cook and sew and launder even if they are also reading Homer or studying Italian painters.

LAURA ASHLEY *on the mindset of her firm*

The only way to grow wise is to be amply idle.

SAUNDERS LEWIS

I'm not working at anything at the moment, but it's steady.

TOMMY COOPER

The last time I was in the unemployment office I told so many lies about wanting to find work they offered me a job in advertising.

RHIANNON EDWARDS

The one power a man can't have stripped from him is the power to do nothing.

MORGAN LLEWELLYN

I never say I'm going to 'play' football. It's work.

MIKE ENGLAND

Laura Ashley's idea of the working woman was one who worked at home.

ANNE SEBBA

Being a footballer is my job and I don't want a day off.

RYAN GIGGS

My first job was a doorman. I kept getting arrested for loitering.

MAX BOYCE

I have led a worthless, wandering and lazy life with, in my early days, a strong dislike to continued labour.

W.H. DAVIES

One of the things I've learned about records – other than that I hate listening to my own ones – is that making them is the easy bit. What's really hard work is promoting them.

CHARLOTTE CHURCH

The idea of a wife with a career was laughable in the 1950s.

SIÂN PHILLIPS

WRITERS AND WRITING

Robert Southey wades through ponderous volumes of travel and old chronicles from which he carefully selects all that is false, useless and absurd. When he has a commonplace book full of monstrosities, he strings them into an epic.

THOMAS LOVE PEACOCK

I never make any attempt to write until it comes to me.

W.H. DAVIES

A country that fears its writers is moribund.

WYN GRIFFITH

Richard Llewelyn has a lot to answer for. He's been responsible for a whole generation of typecasting of the Welsh.

GEORGE PRITCHARD

Authors and uncaptured criminals are the only people free from routine.

ERIC LINKLATER

I fancy they are rather out of touch with reality. By reality I mean shops like Selfridges, motor buses and the *Daily Express*.

T.E. LAWRENCE *on expatriate writers*

Being a novelist these days has almost nothing going for it. In terms of money and social status you would probably be far better off as a tea plantation worker in Sri Lanka.

TOM DAVIES

Most writing is re-writing.

R.S. THOMAS

Being plagiarised felt as if I had walked into my house and found a complete stranger in the kitchen helping himself to a beer from my fridge.

KEN FOLLETT

If to be fulfilled as a writer is to be read then I can't complain.

DICK FRANCIS

Jeffrey Archer can't write fiction and he can't write non-fiction so he's invented a bogus category in between.

IAN HISLOP

It's a novelist's privilege to be unfaithful to the society to which he belongs.

KATE ROBERTS

To read the most passionate of his stories is to live again those long-healed-over moments when we felt on our shrinking flesh and sickened brain the primal revelations of the horrors that stalk the world.

GWYN JONES *on Caradoc Evans*

Anybody can go the way of Dylan Thomas, just sliding down that river of shit. The idea is creation, not adulation. The idea is a man in a room alone, hacking away at a stone and not sucking at the tits of the crowd.

CHARLES BUKOWSKI

To be more interested in the writer than the writing is just eternal human vulgarity.

MARTIN AMIS

Sodom-hipped young men with the inevitable side-whiskers and cigarettes, the faulty livers and the stained teeth, reading Lawrence as an aphrodisiac, spewing onto paper their ignorance and perversions, wetting the bed of their brains with discharges of fungoid verse; this is the art of today.

DYLAN THOMAS

When you have two languages it's hard to write creatively in any one of them.

BETHAN KILFOIL

Bad writing had as much influence on my stuff as good. Writing is a somatic activity at the moment of gestation. Too much thought clogs the works. You end up being able to justify every comma but you bore the pants off everyone.

GREG CULLEN

A born writer is born scrofulous. His career is an accident dictated by physical or circumstantial disabilities.

DYLAN THOMAS

The future of Wales is in the inkbottle.

RICHARD DONES

My father [Kingsley] had severe doubts about the Booker Prize but they evaporated after he heard that he'd actually won it.

MARTIN AMIS

Everyone who writes their autobiography reinvents the past.

DAI WILLIAMS

Dylan hated intellectualising his work. One time someone asked him to explain his poem 'Ballad of the Long-Legged Bait' and he replied, 'It's a description of a gigantic f★★★'.

CAITLIN THOMAS

Erich Segal was never forgiven for writing *Love Story*, a book that outsold the Bible when it was on the bestseller list. He committed the cardinal sin: he had written a fantastic commercial success and he hadn't spent ten years in a garret doing it. And to make matters worse, he was a professor at Yale. Why, the bastard even took baths.

RAY MILLAND

GENERAL SPECULATIONS

One starts life by thinking that civilisation is turning trees into books and finishes it by thinking that a tree is better as a tree.

RICHARD BOOTH

The truth is more important than the facts.

FRANK LLOYD WRIGHT

The sense of being offended is the only creative gesture left to nine people in ten.

GWYN THOMAS

Art is an accident of craft.

DYLAN THOMAS

No one gossips about other people's secret virtues.

BERTRAND RUSSELL

Nobody in show business can ever predict what's going to happen when we go out to face the public. If we did, everyone would be a star and there would be no supporting acts.

HARRY SECOMBE

Every woman turns into her mother eventually.

GLYN ROBERTS

A lie can be halfway around the world before truth has got its boots on.

JAMES CALLAGHAN

The strongest of all psychic forces in the world is unsatisfied desire.

JOHN COWPER POWYS

To forget is to betray.

SAUNDERS LEWIS

Statistically, the probability of any one of us being here is so small you'd think the mere fact of existing would keep us all in a contented dazzlement of surprise.

LEWIS THOMAS

Carl Llewellyn is so optimistic he'd give himself a 50–50 chance after a decapitation.

RICHARD EDMONDSON

Men who are unhappy, like men who sleep badly, are always proud of the fact.

BERTRAND RUSSELL

The truth is more important than the facts.

FRANK LLOYD WRIGHT

People who throw kisses are hopelessly lazy.

BOB HOPE

True beauty lies in that which is undestroyable – and therefore in very little.

DYLAN THOMAS

There is a kind of beauty in defeat.

TERRY GRIFFITHS

It is easy to solve the problems of the world from a soapbox.

DAVID LLOYD GEORGE

Every torturer knows the way to make a man betray himself.

MALCOLM PRYCE

The power to forget is sometimes as important as the power to remember.

ELIZABETH HARRISON

A guest with no arse to his trousers should not complain about a small hole in the tablecloth.

BRIAN WOOD

Everyone has not only a story but a scream.

RACHEL ROBERTS

To win a war is as disastrous as to lose one.

AGATHA CHRISTIE

I'd be a wonderful sugar daddy to some little queen down in Kensington.

DAVID BOWIE

The future is something which everyone reaches at the rate of 60 minutes an hour, whatever he does, wherever he is.

C.S. LEWIS

Shampoo sachets are made of a special indestructible material which can only be torn apart by the teeth at precisely that moment when the shower suddenly goes cold.

MAX BOYCE

I'm haunted by Picasso just as in my youth I was haunted by ghost stories.

CERI RICHARDS

Why is it that wrong numbers are never engaged?

DAFYDD JENKINS

I'm not denying women are foolish. God Almighty made them to match the men.

GEORGE ELIOT

The Philosophical Society of Upper Corris met to discuss the question, 'Is There Life Before Death?'

WYNFORD JONES

There are two kinds of people in the world – those who divide the world into two kinds of people and those who don't.

ROBERT BENCHLEY

The world is becoming like a lunatic asylum run by lunatics.

DAVID LLOYD GEORGE *in 1933*

Culture would not be culture if it were not an acquired taste.

JOHN COWPER POWYS

War doesn't determine who's right, only who's left.

BERTRAND RUSSELL

There's a fine line between bravery and suicide.

TERRY VENABLES

Dying is easy, it's comedy that's hard.

EDMUND GWENN

Why let the truth spoil a good story?

HENRY WILCOXON

I've learned to make disappointment my friend. If you do it allows different opportunities to arise.

RACHEL GRIFFITHS

I have a feeling that the moon until quite recently was a flowering and sensitive planet. Having a good view of the earth it lost all wish to remain a sentient part of the solar system and became the ashen and indifferent lump we now know it to be.

GWYN THOMAS

When the last pit dies, the community spirit will die with it.

PAUL WATKINS

My epitaph, if I ever have one, will be: 'What the hell was all that about?'

ANTHONY HOPKINS

Any insomniac with an important decision to make in the morning knows better than to follow the advice, 'Sleep on it'.

ANNA SWAN

Every cause is personal.

MAGGIE PRYCE JONES

A well is never so full of fresh water that it wouldn't be bettered by a trickle.

TOMMY FARR

Fearful as reality is, it is less fearful than evasions of reality.

CAITLIN THOMAS

Every policeman knows this truth: there is no limit to the things that people will do to other people.

MALCOLM PRYCE

Pity is very near contempt.

SAUNDERS LEWIS

There's always someone worse off than you. Always. And if there isn't, you can comfort yourself with the knowledge that someone else is gaining strength and comfort from looking at you and thinking that at least there's someone worse off than them.

KEITH BARRET

Prison is funny. The minutes drag but the months and years fly by.

HOWARD MARKS

The most dangerous job in the world is held by the man who has to put the first cone out in the fast lane of the A1.

LEE EVANS

Doctrines are the vultures of principle, feeding on it after it's dead.

DAVID LLOYD GEORGE

Nobody deserves to be booed – except Myra Hindley and Anne Robinson.

GLYN WISE

The shortest distance between two points of view is a straight lie.

BETTE DAVIS

Civilisation and syphilisation have advanced together.

ANTHONY HOPKINS

Culture is ordinary. That is where we must start.

RAYMOND WILLIAMS

The world is unbalanced unless we little muts stand together all the time in a more or less unintelligible haze of daftness.

DYLAN THOMAS

The past is the only dead thing that smells sweet.

EDWARD THOMAS

Much of my life has been a circus, played out in full view of the public. And to be honest, I've loved every terrible minute of it.

RICHARD BURTON

Welsh Rarebits is just one of a whole range of publications from Y Lolfa. For a full list of books currently in print, send now for your free copy of our new full-colour catalogue. Or simply surf into our website

www.ylolfa.com

for secure on-line ordering.

y|Lolfa

TALYBONT CEREDIGION CYMRU SY24 5HE
e-mail ylolfa@ylolfa.com
website www.ylolfa.com
phone (01970) 832 304
fax 832 782